FREEDOM FROM STRESS

Books by Edward E. Ford:

Freedom from Stress *

Love Guaranteed: A Better Marriage in Eight Weeks *

Choosing to Love: A New Way to Respond *

Permanent Love: Practical Steps to a Lasting Relationship (with Steven L. Englund) *

Why Marriage?

Why Be Lonely? (with Robert L. Zorn)

For the Love of Children (with Steven L. Englund) *

Money Isn't Enough (with Jim Soldani)

Chapters by the author in:

What Are You Doing?: How People Are Helped Through Reality Therapy. Naomi Glasser, editor. Harper & Row, 1980.

Family Counseling and Therapy. Arthur M. Horne and Merle M. Ohlsen, editors. F.E.Peacock, 1982.

Volitional Action. Wayne Hershberger, editor. North-Holand, 1989.

* Available from:
Brandt Publishing
10209 North 56th Street
Scottsdale, Arizona 85253
602-991-4860

FREEDOM FROM STRESS

most people deal with symptoms. . .
this book, based on perceptual control theory,
deals with causes

Revised Edition

Edward E. Ford, M.S.W.

Foreword by William T. Powers

Brandt Publishing

Cover Design: Dorothy Ford Johnson
Photograph: Michael Balzano
Printing & Packaging: Arrowhead Press, Inc., Phoenix, AZ

Library of Congress Catalog Card Number: 89-91023

ISBN: 0-9616716-1-0

Printed in the United States of America

5   4   3   2   1

Brandt Publishing
10209 North 56th Street
Scottsdale, AZ 85253
602-991-4860

CONTENTS

To William T. Powers
friend and teacher

ACKNOWLEDGEMENTS

Perceptual Control Theory is the heart of this book, and William T. Powers, author of *Behavior: The Control of Perception*, is the leading exponent and contributor to this theory today. He and his fellow scientists, members of the Control Systems Group*, continue to research and publish their papers in various scientific journals. Members of the group who are not scientists, such as myself, attempt to make these ideas practical for the general public. If it weren't for Bill Powers, this book would not have been written.

I dedicated this book to him because of the person, Bill Powers. Underneath the genius of this man is a very beautiful individual. He is a man possessed of great patience, of gentle confidence and humility, who is willing to spend hours with persons such as myself as we struggle to understand this most complex of theories. I especially appreciate Bill's consent to my request to write the foreword to this book.

Mary Powers, Bill's wife, has been most helpful. Like her husband, her support and kindness to all of us who work with Bill to bring these ideas to others is a reflection of her own inner dedication to her husband and his ideas.

There are many who have helped. Principal among them is Tracy Ryan, a student of mine at the graduate School of Social Work, Arizona State University. She helped make Bob and Betty, the characters you will meet in this book, come alive and offered many valuable, detailed suggestions throughout the many revisions of this manuscript — right up until the end. She made this effort most enjoyable.

Experimental psychologist Tom Bourbon was most helpful in his several reviews and his feedback of my manuscript. So was Bill Williams, a writer and researcher in economics from Boulder, Colorado.

My sister, Amy Weden from Weston, Massachusetts, really worked hard on the manuscript. Twice she reviewed it, and her penetrating questions and insightful comments helped me to raise the quality of my work to a much higher level. Others contributed to this manuscript: Jim Soldani, a management consultant from Phoenix, who challenged much of what I said and forced me to do a little more thinking; David Goldstein, a clinical psychologist from Cherry Hill, New Jersey; Brent Dennis, assistant professor, Social Work Department, Bowling Green State University in Ohio; Harry Hollack, general manager with Intel Corporation; Ruth Welch, a close family friend, who gave valuable information on alcoholism; Bonnie Briglia from Phoenix; Gary Applegate, PhD, founder of the Center for Skill Development, Sherman Oaks, California, and author of *Happiness: It's Your Choice*, for the idea of the "wants" activity in Chapter 6; and my graduate students who challenge my thinking and rarely let me get away with anything. Appreciation is due my close friend, Frederic J. Shaw, JD, PhD, who edited several final versions with a great deal of care and precision. I also thank my daughter, Dorothy, for the nice job she did on the cover design. And I am deeply appreciative to Wayne Paulson of Alpha Communications, New Brighton, Minnesota, for taking my manuscript and producing my publication.

I thank Dag Forssell for his enthusiastic support of my work and especially for his help in both identifying editing errors in the first edition of this book and providing suggestions for Appendix 2 of this edition. My sincere appreciation goes to Greg Williams, who edited Appendix 2 and compiled Appendix 3, which lists major references on Perceptual Control Theory. As Archivist for the Control Systems Group, Greg's dedication to preserving the important work in PCT is a major contribution.

I have been a very fortunate man. I couldn't have had better parents. I have wonderful — although at times slightly crazy — children, all eight of them. Now they are producing delightful grandchildren. To Hester, all I can say is that I love you. Thanks for hanging in.

*For information, contact:

CSG Newsletter, 10209 N. 56th St., Scottsdale, AZ 85253. Phone (602)991-4860.

CSG Book Publishing, 460 Black Lick Rd., Gravel Switch, KY 40328. Phone (606)332-7606.

CSG Business Office, 73 Ridge Pl., CR 510, Durango, CO 81301. Phone (303)247-7986.

FOREWORD

William T. Powers

Ed Ford is a charter member of an odd collection of scientists and professionals called the Control Systems Group. The basic theme that holds this group together is a conception of human behavior that grew out of cybernetics in the early 1950s. For many years, *perceptual control theory* (as the new idea is called, at least by me, this week) was nursed along and developed by a very small handful of people. It wasn't very popular among psychologists for two main reasons. The first was that it sounded too much like engineering and not enough like real people. The second was that when most psychologists began to get a glimmer of what it is about, they would slam the door and pull the shutters closed. It was perfectly clear that if the concepts in perceptual control theory are right, not much that psychologists have believed would survive.

Slowly, however, understanding of this new idea spread. The main lines of development still didn't look very promising as a realistic picture of how people work, because the experiments being done were very simple, tending to involve a person sitting in front of a computer screen wiggling a joystick. There were, however, a few people like Ed who kept insisting that perceptual control theory – or just control theory for short – had to be made understandable to everyone, not just to mathematicians, engineers, and psychologists. When Ed got tired of insisting, he decided he would have to do it himself. That is how this book and the one that preceded it came into existence.

Ed is not an amateur, but a Master of Social Work with a long history of experience as a successful counselor. But his background was in practical dealings with human affairs, not with abstract theories. His own struggles to translate ideas from one world into another for himself have turned into a growing skill in translating those ideas into common and understandable terms.

That is why he is a valued member of a group that is rather heavy with abstract thinkers and academic types. Ed's role is to make these people explain clearly and simply what they mean, often with the result that they come to understand their own ideas better. After he has made them do this, he turns around and writes books like *Freedom from Stress*. The academics in the Control Systems Group might look at a book of this sort and say, "Well, I wouldn't write it that way." After they read it carefully, however, they must admit that all the ideas are there, properly expressed, sounding like nothing more than good common sense. I think this is quite an achievement. I also think that Ed attests to one of the main strengths of the Control Systems Group: it is free of intellectual snobbery, demonstrating through work like that of Ed's the advantages of openness.

Stress is often described in a way that makes it sound something like measles – a disease that you catch, something that gets inside you and causes troubles like an invading microorganism. The principles of control theory, however, teach us that human beings and other organisms are complex systems run more by inner motivations and networks of goals than by external forces. They are so complex that they can get themselves into trouble, one part of the whole system coming into conflict with another part. Control theorists think that stress is a condition in which a person is at war internally, one desire thwarting another desire, one goal canceling another goal. A human being, in other words, creates the stress in an attempt to deal with the problems of life in a way that's not internally consistent.

It's not pleasant to be told, in effect, "You're doing it to yourself." But from another point of view, that is a very encouraging judgment – if you're doing it to yourself, then you can also stop doing it to yourself. The catch, of course, is that you're not aware of doing this to yourself; if you were, you wouldn't have the problem because then you would just stop doing whatever is clearly causing the problem. If you're doing it to yourself, but don't see how, this means that you have to learn something about how your body and mind work. Only then can you see the indirect and subtle ways in which inner conflict can arise; then you can change the goals and perceptions that led to the conflict that generates the symptoms we call stress.

Ed's aim in this book is first to teach control theory in terms that are relevant to ordinary life and the problems of real people who aren't theoreticians. That's the main theme in his current writings. But in this book he slants the message toward the specific problem of stress: what it is and what people can do to free themselves of this difficulty. He is convinced, and I agree, that the basic task is to understand what is going on, not to prescribe some pill or procedure that will work like a cold remedy. Out of understanding will come awareness of what has to change. And then the change will come about naturally.

Control theory is not the perfect final answer to everything; it simply represents what many reasonable people think is the best current guess about how we work. Ed tells you here enough about this theory so you can make up your own mind, check out what he says for yourself. No book can substitute for a personal relationship with a helpful and experienced counselor, but this book may give you a head start in solving the kinds of problems meant by the word *stress*.

"They are called wise who put things
in their right order and control them well"
Thomas Aquinas (1225-1274)
Summa Contra Gentiles

INTRODUCTION

Most books on stress deal with its physiological symptoms – high blood pressure, stomach upset, stiff necks, back pain, headaches, inability to relax, insomnia – and with the subsequent feelings of anxiety, irritability, anger, depression, and tension. These symptoms are real and very painful. This book, on the other hand, describes the causes of those stress symptoms and what we can do about them. Presented here are solutions that offer struggling human beings ways to restore internal harmony within their own lives, regardless of the environment in which they find themselves – whether at work, at home, or elsewhere.

At the very heart of this book is perceptual control theory, which is a complex model for describing how people think and why they behave as they do. Control theory teaches that we create our own unique world through a hierarchy of control systems and store them in our memory. From these created perceptions, we build our own systems of values and standards, which form the basis for how we make decisions and deal with both ourselves and others so that we can create satisfying lives.

Unlike other theories, control theory is concerned solely with feedback, that is, the result of our actions, not with the actions themselves. Our system of values and standards continually operates as a closed-loop control system to satisfy our internal goals by trying to reduce the difference between what we want and how we perceive the outcome of our efforts, which is the input.

We always deal with the external world to satisfy our own internal goals, never the goals of others. Regardless of what happens to us as we interact with the environment, the ultimate reason for our actions is our attempts to satisfy our own individually-set values, priorities, and standards. No one else creates our goals – nor sets them. We do.

Most behavioral scientists teach otherwise. These scientists don't think in terms of a closed-loop system. They see the perceptual inputs as causing the organism to produce behavioral outputs. Stimulus simply produces response. They recognize that actions do have effects on future stimulation, but they see this as something separate, not a part of one single process. Frankly, I've never believed we are at the whim of what happens to us. My study of control theory has confirmed this suspicion.

What all this means is that we are responsible for what we do. It is not our parents, not drugs or alcohol, not the pressure of our friends, not our feelings, not the seductive advances of others, not the product we bought, not the hot weather or the freezing temperature, not the Good Lord, not the media, not our job, not our spouse or children, not the other driver, and certainly not a thing called *stress*. The bottom line is that we are the captains of our own ships.

We live in a culture that has been taken in by excuse-makers. We keep trying to find out why we are the way we are. This constant searching leads us through a maze of endless pathways. The fact is that we are not diseased when we act irresponsibly. Feelings do not cause us to act foolishly. No medicine or operation is going to cure a lifetime of bad eating, excessive drinking or drugging, and lack of exercise. Someone yelling and screaming does not cause us to be upset. The solution is obvious. We must look to the one source of all stress: our own self-made conflicting goals or impossible desires. It is our ability to maintain harmony throughout the whole network of values we've built, priorities we've established, standards we've set, and decisions we've made that will bring us the most satisfaction in life.

As long as we look outwardly for reasons for our unhappiness, we will remain miserable. Fortunately, internal peace is possible. All we have to do is to examine the world that we have constructed, reflect on what is really important to us, critically review our values, look at how we've set our priorities, set forth standards that reflect these values, and begin to make decisions that are based on our own standards. If our own values and standards don't bring us the peace we want, we had better re-evaluate our entire system. Eventually, with a little help from above, we will find this internal harmony. The two characters in this book, Bob and Betty, reflect such an attempt. I've worked with hundreds who have succeeded.

As in my recent book, *Love Guaranteed,* I have used a counseling format for this book. That is, you will encounter my application of control theory to the problem of stress through counseling sessions with a ficticious couple. Bob and Betty represent a cross section of the kinds of problems I deal with in both my private counseling practice as well as those problems presented to me by my students in my classes at Arizona State University's School Of Social Work.

Freedom from Stress reveals much about my approach to the task of counseling. It is evident that, as a counselor, I see myself primarily as a teacher. If I am to be true to the premises of control theory, I must teach people how to change their lives on their own. With respect to this theory, I often find myself swimming upstream in the counseling profession. Most counselors use much different and more accepted methods. Were it not for the effectiveness I experience with my approach, I might worry about that.

I usually see people who present problems such as Betty's and Bob's for two to three months. I see many other clients only two or three times. I work with a few for many months – sometimes years.

Although I teach my clients elements of control theory in our sessions, it must be said that I don't attempt to be as thorough as I am with Bob and Betty in this book. That thoroughness is for your benefit as the reader and as a fellow explorer of the application of control theory to human concerns. With clients, I teach what is needed for them to make the changes they want to make.

The smaller diagrams that I present Bob and Betty throughout the book all relate to the complete Control Theory diagram found in Appendix 1. Once you begin to understand the concepts, you will want to refer to the complete chart to understand their inter-relationships.

If you are interested in the concept of quality time presented in Chapter 4, a more detailed explanation can be found in my book, *Love Guaranteed: A Better Marriage in Eight Weeks* (Brandt Publishing, 1987). Similarly, more discussion of the idea of social maturity of children, found in Chapter 9, appears in my book *For the Love of Children* (Brandt Publishing, 1977), Chapters 1 and 7.

Finally, if you would like to obtain free copies of the Quality Time (Love), Teaching Responsibility, Counseling, and Freedom from Stress 3X5 cards referred to in this book, send a stamped, self-addressed envelope with your request to Brandt Publishing.

Edward E. Ford, M.S.W.
Phoenix, Arizona
March 7, 1989

Chapter 1

MISERY

"Bob? Come on in. Please sit down." I gestured to a chair. "What can I do for you?"

Bob slumped down in the chair opposite mine. "At this point, I don't know where to begin or even if anyone can help me. I'm so stressed out! I just don't know what to do. I've got problems at home, problems at work. I'm miserable all the time."

"You've come to the right place, Bob," I said reassuringly. "I teach people how to deal with their problems."

"That's what Jim said," Bob commented hopefully. "He's my brother. He said you were different."

"What do you do for a living?"

"Well, if you ask my boss – not very much," Bob answered. "He's one of the problems. I have a boss who is never satisfied – constantly on my back criticizing what I do and what I haven't done."

"What do you do?"

"I'm plant manager at Willard Manufacturing," he replied. "We make electrical components for various manufacturers and contractors. My boss is vice president of operations for the company."

"Do you like the kind of work you do?"

"It's all right, I guess. It's a job, but I don't enjoy it like I used to. Besides, no one wants to work any more. Not only do I have trouble with my boss, I'm also fed up with my employees. They always have an excuse for everything. I've tried yelling at them, criticizing them, and even playing Mr. Nice Guy. Nothing works."

"What's your situation at home?"

"Worse," he said, frustration showing in his voice. "Betty and I have really drifted apart over the past few years."

"You are married to Betty?"

"Yeah, if you want to call it that," he said bitterly. "All she does is whine about how I don't care about her anymore. I find myself disliking just about everything she does. Lately, I just try to stay out of her way. She keeps threatening me with divorce, but she just hangs in there. We've been married twenty-four years. She's a branch manager at National Bank. You'd think we'd be happy after all these years."

"Any children?"

"Four. The oldest is my twenty-three-year-old son, Mike, who drinks too much and can't ever seem to find a job. When he does, he can't hang on to it. Nothing motivates that stupid kid! He's living with his girl friend, Marsha. She's got a good job with an accounting firm and goes to Phoenix College. I have no idea why she puts up with him.

"Next is June, my twenty-two-year-old daughter. She's a Junior at the University of Arizona and is doing pretty well. She's working as a waitress this summer. Her problem is this idiot boyfriend of hers. What a loser! I just can't understand why she would go for a such a person.

"Then there's Tim. He's fifteen, but acts like a ten-year-old. His mother gives in to him on everything. I hardly ever see him. God knows what he's into.

"Finally, there is Ruthie. She's eight and a real sweetheart. She seems to be having some difficulties in school, but she'll work them out. She's always after me to do things, likes to crawl up into my lap, and wants me to play a card game with her. She loves Crazy Eights. She is the one bright spot in my life."

"Are there any other areas of your life that bother you?"

"No, not unless you count my migraine headaches. I've been going to doctors for the past three years, and none of them has been able to find out what's wrong. They all say it's stress, but no one tells me what to do about it. I've been taking pills, but nothing helps."

"Any other area?" I asked.

"Isn't that enough?" he snapped. "Anything else and I would fall apart. No one understands what I've been through. It seems like none of my family or my boss really care." He looked down at the floor, thought for a moment, and then added, "No one really cares."

"What area is of most concern to you – your problem with Betty, your children, or your difficulties at work?"

"I feel so completely at a loss, I just don't know what to do," Bob replied, not hearing my question. "I've got this friend at work, Luke. He has worse problems than I have, but he seems to handle them much better. His wife left him two years ago. She just disappeared. He's been taking care of her two kids – they're not even his! They're her kids by another marriage. He's got the boss on his back a lot more than I have. He's the quality control supervisor. Yet he goes around, always pleasant to everyone. I don't know how Luke does it."

"Would you be interested in learning how he does it?"

"I don't understand," Bob replied.

"Would you be interested in learning how Luke is able to deal with all of his problems and stay calm and pleasant despite the circumstances? You're all upset and miserable, and he isn't."

"Well, if you could just tell me how to get my boss off my back and get a few foremen who were willing to work, maybe things would be better," Bob answered.

"Bob, did you hear what you just said?" I asked.

"No, what did I say?" he answered, sounding confused.

"You just told me that your boss and employees need straightening out, yet you also admitted that Luke, who has it worse at home than you do, is able to handle the same problems you have at work." Bob looked at me, and again I said, "Are you interested in learning how Luke is able to deal with everything around him and still remain calm and pleasant?"

"You know how to keep a person focused, don't you?" he said, smiling for the first time.

"You're paying me for something," I replied, smiling back.

"The last guy I went to had me talking about my feelings and all the family problems I've been having," he said. "After three months and eight hundred bucks, I decided he was the only one who was benefiting from the counseling. I was ready to give up on you guys until my brother told me about you."

"Bob, are you interested in learning Luke's secret for handling his problems while still remaining calm?" I asked again.

"Yes, I am," he replied. "You certainly keep things on track. We could use you in our plant meetings."

"What do you think is Luke's secret?"

"I don't know," he said slowly. He continued thoughtfully, "I guess he doesn't let others get to him – you know what I mean? He doesn't let others get him upset."

"Do you think others cause you to be the way you are?"

"What do you mean?" he asked.

"Is it your boss or your wife and kids that cause you to be upset?"

"Well, sure, they all do," he replied. "I'd be happy as hell if they would treat me better."

"You just told me that you and Luke are treated the same by your boss, perhaps Luke a little worse, and you both have problems in your family life, yet Luke seems happier and less stressed out than you. Is that because of the way he is treated?"

"No, I suppose he looks at things a lot differently," he answered.

"So, what we do isn't caused by what happens to us, but rather by how we view things. Is that what you're saying?"

"I guess so, but I'm getting confused," he said, looking puzzled. "Somehow I've always figured that we can't control things like stress. Are you saying I can control it?"

"Bob, let me show you something that should help you understand what I'm saying," I said, holding up my hand. "Raise your right hand up, palm facing me, like you would if you were taking an oath in a courtroom." I placed the palm of my hand against Bob's hand and applied a small amount of pressure. Bob's hand went back about a foot, and then he held firm.

"Let's try that again, Bob." We did it twice more. The second time his hand didn't budge when I applied the same pressure. The third time he pushed back, and my hand retreated about six inches.

"Bob, what caused your hand to go back when I pushed it?"

"Well, you did," he replied.

"Then why didn't it work the second and third time?"

"Because I didn't want you pushing it back," he answered. Then he looked at me and grinned. "I guess I caused my own hand to go back the first time because I didn't resist you."

"Did I determine where your hand went, or did you?"

"I did," he said slowly. "You know, that's kind of interesting. I always thought that when someone does something and I get mad, it's the other person's fault. I don't know, this is all sort of confusing."

"Would you be interested in learning how we control what we do, especially how we perceive things?"

"Yes, I guess so," he answered, "but will that help me with my problems?"

"Are you in control of getting what you want?" I asked.

"No, I guess not," Bob said, looking down at the floor. "I'm not really in control of anything. That's my problem. So what do you mean about learning how to control?"

"The more you understand about how you function as a human being, especially how your brain works, the easier it is to learn how to take control of your life, to find some degree of happiness, and to deal effectively with others. The stress you've been experiencing is evidence of that lack of control and of internal conflicts within your system. Once you learn how to take control of your life, you can remain calm and collected in the face of adversity – just like Luke does."

"That makes sense," he said, nodding.

"In order to understand the cause of stress and how to deal with it, you first have to understand how the brain works." I stood up and moved to the chalkboard on the wall. "I want you to try an exercise with me. Here are two rubber bands, tied together by a single knot. I'm placing a dot on this chalkboard, and I want you to try to keep the knot directly over the dot on the chalkboard. I'll hold the end of one rubber band. You hold this chalk, which I have placed inside the other rubber band. Then, when I move my rubber band, you try to keep the knot over the dot on the board by moving your rubber band. Your movements will be recorded on the board since your chalk is held against the board."

Bob put the chalk and rubber band against the chalkboard and looked at me dubiously.

"Are you ready?"

"Yeah, I guess so," he answered.

As I moved the end of my rubber band up and down, closer and further away from the dot, Bob began moving his rubber band, attempting to keep the knot between the two over the dot. The piece of chalk traced a record of his movements.

"O.K., let's discuss what just happened. First, what did you want to do in this exercise?"

"I wanted to keep the knot over the dot," he said.

I wrote a big **W** next to the dot. "And how did you know that you were doing this?"

"Well, I looked at the distance between the knot and the dot and moved the rubber band to keep the knot as close as possible to the dot."

"That's right," I said, as I wrote a large **P** on the board next to the **W** and drew a circle around both. "This scribbling you did with the chalk represents your attempt to maintain the harmony between what you wanted, which was to keep the knot over the dot, and what you perceived, which was how far the knot was from the dot. The erratic chalk lines reflect your actions.

"Suppose a person saw these chalk marks but didn't know what you wanted, what do you think the impression of your actions would be?"

"That I was a little crazy," Bob replied, grinning.

"Do you think that person could have told you exactly what you had wanted and what you were perceiving?"

"Well, no, how could anyone tell by just looking at those scribbles?" Bob replied, looking mystified.

"Those scribbles represent your actions, what you did so that you could achieve what you wanted – to keep the knot over the dot on the board. Do you think it's possible for you to know all the things people have in their minds when you see them doing something?" I asked.

"Of course not," Bob said, shaking his head. "I'd just be assuming a lot of things. If someone had seen what I was doing there on the board, I'm sure that person would have thought I was half nuts."

"Once people understand what you want, do you think there is a difference in how they perceive you?".

"Well, sure, there would have to be a difference. They would understand what was going on, you know, what you were thinking," Bob replied.

"Were you aware of the marks you were making as we were doing this exercise?"

"No, not really," he answered. "I was concentrating on keeping the knot over the dot."

"This exercise is a simple explanation of how the brain works." I pointed to the erratic marks he had made while moving his rubber band and continued, "Most people are continually trying to change their own or another's actions or behaviors. Yet we rarely think about what we are actually doing. What causes our actions is our attempt to correct the difference between what we want and how we perceive we're doing." I pointed to the circled **W** and **P**. "And that's what we are going to deal with in this office – what you want and how you perceive things. As either of those change, your actions will change accordingly."

"I'm still a little confused," Bob said, looking puzzled. "Are you saying we don't think about what we are doing?"

I returned to my chair and motioned for Bob to sit down. "Did you think of what you were doing in this exercise, or were you watching the knot in relation to the dot?"

"I'm beginning to understand," he responded thoughtfully.

"Let me use a common experience as an example, Bob. Supposing you wanted to drive forty-five miles per hour, how would you know you are accomplishing what you wanted?"

"By checking the speedometer," Bob replied.

"Do you ever think, when you decide to go a certain speed, about how hard your foot should be pressing against the accelerator?"

"No, of course not. I automatically know how hard to push," he said, shrugging his shoulders. "I don't consciously think of it."

"And do you ever think of how you move the steering wheel when you want to keep your car centered in your lane?"

"No, I just look to see where my car is in relationship to the lines on the road," he answered.

"Anytime we act in any way, we're conscious of two things: **what we want** and **the results of what we are doing**. That's a condensed picture of how the mind works."

"Don't we ever think about what we're doing?" Bob asked.

"Rarely. Whether it's driving a car, typing a letter, or combing our hair, people are designed so that we always consciously look at the results of our actions – not at the actions themselves.

"It's what the mind *wants* that determines where its attention is directed. Unless we make a conscious effort to look at specific actions, we rarely think about what we are doing. Even then, we have trouble. Programming or reprogramming our actions involves a lot of work – looking at specific actions and comparing them with the actual physical motions that we want to perceive ourselves doing or saying. For example, learning to type, to play a musical instrument, or to develop a golf swing are all attempts to program specific behavioral patterns that will achieve what we want. Developing and then programming new muscle actions is not easy. But, once they are learned, we just give a thought command to our systems and the muscle program connected with what we want is activated. Actually, the less conscious we become of our actions, the more proficient we become."

"Why is that?" he asked.

"Because we rarely think of what we do when we want something, as in the rubber band experiment we just did. When I take a shower or fix a meal, I don't think of the actual movements of my hands and arms. I literally watch myself accomplish what I want, without much thought as to the specific muscle movements. Changing actual muscle coordinations is possible, but the most efficient way to do that is through consciously thinking about what we want and our perceptions, just as I showed you in the rubber band demonstration.

"The same principles hold true for a person's relationships. I'm sure you are quite capable of being kind and loving to your wife. You probably acted that way when you were first dating and early in your marriage. As time passed, you probably came to perceive Betty somewhat differently than when you were courting her. Also, I'm sure the various things you want have changed. The way to reactivate those kind and loving actions is by altering your perception of Betty and developing a stronger commitment to her. A change in your actions will naturally follow."

"Well, I don't know what I have to look at to get my life straightened out, but I do need help, that's for sure," Bob said, sitting back in the chair. "So, where do we go from here?"

"You mentioned a few minutes ago that no one understood what you're going through and how unhappy you are, right?"

"Right," he said.

"So what is it that you want?"

"Well, I guess I want to feel better about myself," he said quietly. "I guess what I really want is to have less stress at work, you know, to be happier at work, to feel competent and respected. Also, I want to feel closer to my family and get along with them better."

"You mentioned that you weren't getting along with your boss, arguing with him all the time, and that you yell, criticize, and occasionally play Mr. Nice Guy around your employees. Are all these actions helping you get what you want at work?"

"Hell, no! They only make things worse," he said emphatically.

"And with your family, you mentioned that you criticized Betty a lot and now you try to avoid her. Also, you have little or no contact with Tim – I believe you said you never saw him. Is what you are doing at home helping you get closer to your family?"

"No, apparently not. Things are getting worse there as well." He then added quietly, "Much worse."

"Would you like to work at making things better?"

"Yeah, I guess so," he said.

"Bob, are you really serious about working at improving your job and your family life?" I asked, not totally convinced by his first response.

Tears began to fill his eyes. He looked at me and said, "I've got to make things better. I don't have any other choice. I've been so on edge lately. I thought I had achieved everything I wanted. You know, a good job, a family, nice home, boat, club memberships, and yet I'm miserable. My stomach hurts, I can't sleep at night, my headaches are killing me, and work is pure agony. I used to enjoy going to work.

"Then, there is my family. I don't want to lose Betty. I really do care about her, you know. I don't have the faintest idea how to deal with my kids. I just feel so alone all the time. I need help figuring out what to do."

"O.K., Bob, I believe you. And you came to the right place. I can teach you."

Chapter 2

THE MAKING OF OUR OWN WORLD

"First, Bob, I'd like to know those things that are important to you. Let me list them here on the chalkboard."

"What do you mean?" he asked.

"I'd like to hear from you all those things that you consider important in your life."

"Well, being successful at my job is very important," he began, "I need the money. Having good mental and physical health is critical, and I get that through sports. So, sports are important. Obviously, my family life, my wife and kids, they should be on the list. Then there's my parents, my older brother, kid sister, and my friends. I guess I would include a nice house."

"Okay, Bob," I said, writing the list on my chalkboard. "Is there anything else that comes to your mind?"

"No," he answered. "I guess that's about it."

"Now I want you to evaluate this list in order of importance. What would be your top priority?"

"Well, success at work has always been uppermost in my mind," he said. "That would be number one."

"All right, what's second?"

"Well, my health is important," Bob said. "I play golf several times a week and try to stay in shape. I suppose my wife and children should be second, but, if you don't have your health, you aren't much good to your family. Let's make health second and then my wife and children third."

"How about the rest?" I asked.

"I guess they come in the order that you have listed on the board," Bob answered as I jotted down the numbers.

I pointed to the chalkboard. "Is this the way you perceive your priorities?"

Bob's Priorities

1. success at job
2. good health – mental and physical, including sports
3. family life, wife, and kids
4. parents
5. brother
6. sister
7. friends
8. nice house

"I suppose they are my priorities." he said. Bob paused for a moment and then added, "Well, I guess it looks like my family doesn't seem very important to me, does it?"

"These are your priorities, Bob," I answered. "Since you have to live with them, don't you think you should be the judge?"

"Yeah, I guess I should be," he answered, somewhat dejectedly. "I always felt as if work was the most important part of my life. I've always put my work and my health first." He stared at his list. Then, looking at me, he quietly added, "I guess my family really should be more important, shouldn't it?"

"Is there anything wrong with re-evaluating your priorities?"

"No, I guess there isn't," he answered. "I was just thinking about the look on Betty's face this morning when I left for work. She looked a hundred years old. I suppose I've been ignoring her. She is constantly hassled by the kids, and she has very little to look forward to. The more I think about it, the more she should come first. Three years ago, I was in the hospital with a ruptured disk – and guess who was there, every single day, without complaining? Yeah, Betty should come first, then my kids, then my job and health. That's the way my priorities should be set up."

"So what is it that you want to work on first, Bob?   The areas concerning your job, your individual life, your relationship with Betty, or your relationship with any of your children?"

"Betty," he said. "I want to work on making things better between the two of us. It's funny how you can live with someone and yet you feel so lonely when you're around them. We're like two ships passing in the night."

"How do you see me helping you with regard to Betty?"

"I don't know," he said, somewhat surprised by my question. "If only I could get her in here, maybe you could talk to her. Perhaps it would straighten her out. If only she would change her attitude about me. It seems like she's critical all the time."

"Do you think it is possible for you to change Betty?"

"No," he said. "I was sort of hoping you could talk with her."

"So you think it is possible that I could change your wife's attitude and the way she criticizes you?"

"No, I guess not," he said dejectedly. "I try to do things to please her, but somehow nothing ever works out. She's always correcting what I do, telling me what I do wrong. It's hard to get close to people when they're doing that."

"If you can't change her, who can you change?"

"Myself, obviously, but I've tried changing what I do around her, and nothing ever seems to work," he answered. "It's like were both stuck in a rut, and neither of us can get out."

"Has trying to change what you are doing around her helped?"

"No, it hasn't," he replied, showing frustration. "If anything, it seems to make things worse. She isn't satisfied, and I get more upset."

"How about your perception of her, could you change that?"

"How would that help?" he asked.

"When was the last time you were angry at her?"

"Last night," he said. "She tried to correct the way I was talking to Tim. Then she accused me of never listening to her or something like that, and I just told her to get off my back. Then, the next thing you know, we were yelling and screaming at each other."

"How did you perceive her when you blew up at her?"

"You really want to know?" he asked.

"Yes."

"As a cold, stupid bitch," he answered angrily. "And that's exactly what she was – cold and stupid."

"A few minutes ago, you told me you wanted to draw closer to her, that you don't want to lose Betty, and that you really do care. Those were your very words. When you were saying that to me, do you recall how you perceived her at that moment?"

"Yes, I do," he answered, lowering his voice. "I saw her as a warm and loving person."

"Last night, when she was after you about something, suppose you had thought about her as warm and loving, just as you did a few minutes ago. Do you think you would have told her to get off your back?"

"Of course not," Bob said, looking puzzled. "Because..." Then he hesitated and thought for a moment.

"Well, what are you thinking?"

"I would have been a little less harsh, more understanding," he said. Then he added, "I guess you treat people according to how you are thinking about them at the time. I never thought of that before."

"Remember the rubber band demonstration? What we do depends on two things: how we perceive people – or think about them, to use your words – and what we want. If you *want* to be happy with Betty, that's half the battle. The second half is how you *perceive* her."

"When you continually build a strong perception of her as warm and loving, then, when differences do occur, whatever she does will be judged by you in relation to how you perceive her. If you have strong and loving memories of her and you really want her in your life, then the way you deal with what she does will be tempered by your perception of her. It's just that simple."

"I understand what you're saying, but, you know, Ed, our problems are very serious," Bob countered, looking worried. "I think a lot of these problems we've been having need to be talked about and worked through. I just think it's important she knows how I feel."

"You just told me you spent three months and eight hundred dollars doing just that, and it didn't work."

"Well, it's supposed to help." Bob sat looking thoughtful for a moment, then added, "I guess maybe it didn't."

"The key to working out difficulties is to build a strong enough relationship so that you can discuss things reasonably and rationally," I explained. "Also, you will find that, as your perception of the person with whom you are having difficulty improves, many of the so-called problems disappear. You'll discover they were only symptoms of a weak relationship."

"What you're saying about how I perceive her makes sense, but I still don't fully understand," Bob admitted.

"It's confusing at first, but, as you think about these things, it all becomes clearer. It's hard to realize that each of us is dealing in our own unique way with what is being viewed. The problem is that we *are* the perceptual system. We use our senses to construct our perception of the environment within our own brains, and there's nothing outside of ourselves that tells us about the uniqueness of those perceptions. And, because we are totally unaware of what the neural connections in our brains are doing, there's nothing within us that tells us we are manipulating the energy from the outside world as it comes into our brains.

"In other words, your perception of what Betty does and how you organize that energy as it comes in through your perceptual system is strictly your own doing. She can't perceive it happening within you. Nor can you, for that matter. What she was doing didn't correlate with what you wanted, but did correlate with how you perceived her. So you attempted to correct that difference by trying to get her off your back. The action you took was to yell and scream at her.

"If you recall the rubber band demonstration, we rarely think of our actions but rather are very much aware of what we want and our perceptions. If you had held a strong perception of her as warm and loving, her comments to you would have been interpreted in light of that perception, and you would have dealt with what she said as having come from a warm and loving spouse. You would have treated her a little more kindly, I'm sure.

"To help you grasp how all this works, let me first explain how the perceptual system functions. This should help you understand how differently we all perceive the world around us, including the people with whom we work and live.

"In your perceptual system, you create your own individual understanding of the world. The energy which your system senses passes in sequence through a series of very unique controls and slowly develops into the way you understand your environment. This process is somewhat analogous to what happens when you take a picture with a camera which has various functions and a series of lenses attached.

"What gives your picture its individuality is where you point the camera, when you snap the picture, and, probably most important of all, how you manipulate the lens opening, the depth of focus, and each lens. As you adjust all this equipment, you give the picture a reflection of your own personality, of how you think the subject should look, of what you want. Each function has its own peculiar characteristics – whether to filter out light, to add certain colors, or whatever. The final product will always differ in some way from other photographs of the same subject because of your own way of adjusting the apparatus to create what you want. This process of creating a photograph is similar to how each of us constructs our perceptions.

"What gives us our unique view of the world – including other people – is how we each manipulate our own control system, our internal 'camera', if you like. We use these control systems of ours to build an understanding of the world in every given circumstance. Also, these control systems are constantly influenced by the memories we maintain of all our past experiences. In short, we have been endowed with a fascinating system that's designed to help us make sense out of our environments so that we can build a satisfying life for ourselves. After all, we can only want what we have created through our perceptual systems, but we'll talk about what we want later."

"I have an idea that understanding this perceptual system is going to help me solve some of my difficulties at work," Bob said, sounding encouraged. "Everyone talks about the same problems, but no one sees them the same way. It all sounds so simple. How do we perceive things so differently? How do we change our perceptions?"

"The best way to understand all this is to review the characteristics of each of these control levels. These levels of control are the mechanisms which human beings use to process all the energy which is sensed in the environment and is formed into usable information called perceptions. Each level has its own separate characteristics.

"Take a look at this diagram." I handed him a sheet of paper.

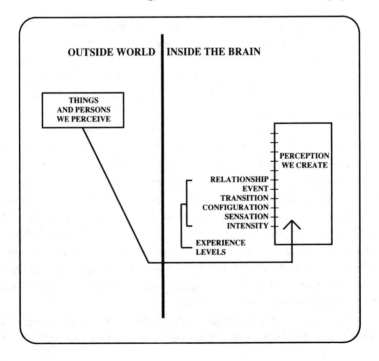

"There are eleven levels, and the best way to learn the first six is to imagine yourself as a small baby. You have not yet begun to form conceptual symbols based on experiences. You don't understand words and concepts. Your only knowledge comes through what you experience, and you remember only these experiences. Thus, even as I define the first six levels, you will see that it's *the experience of sensing the environment* that really characterizes each of them.

"Sensory receptors are our only link with the external world. It's at this first level, called **intensity**, through which all awareness of the environment enters the brain. These receptors include hearing, smelling, seeing, tasting, and the sense of contact when anything in the environment comes in contact with the body. In short, this is where all knowledge begins.

"This first level arranges all the neural currents flowing in through the senses so that the next level that follows can use the information to form an understandable perception. Each level in the series only knows what the prior level tells it. Along with arranging the incoming information, the first level also tells the next level how much energy is coming in. At intensity level, it doesn't know what's coming in, it only experiences how much.

"At the second level, **sensation**, we begin to experience the energy in terms of rough or smooth, bright or dim, loud or soft, hot or cold, and so on. Further understanding of this energy is constructed through some kind of recognizable shape or form at the third level, **configuration**. For example, we create our ideas of food substances through experiencing various sense signals such as taste, smell, texture, temperature, ease of chewing, and its visual appearance at sensation level. Even some sounds are attached to food, like the sound of pop corn or a sizzling steak. But, remember, at this level we haven't called it anything yet. We're only recognizing combinations of sensed energy in patterns and forms.

"Rates of change of any lower perception are understood at the fourth level, called **transition**. Here we visually experience movement, changes in illumination, or in intensity of sound. We experience movement when a ball is thrown at us. We would notice it getting bigger, spinning, and how fast it is coming at us. All this gives us a sense of transition or a change in configuration. Your spouse raises her voice, or you notice the shower water suddenly getting hotter, or your son's radio gets louder.

"At the fifth level, you begin to notice **events** going on all about you. These might be best described as segmented happenings. Daddy and Mommie kiss, your brother ties his shoe, someone opens the door, a ball bounces on the floor, water spills on the table, your father shaves, your mother combs her hair, your sister giggles – all these occurrences take place, and you recognize their continuity.

"Then you perceive an object and, even though you can't yet conceptually identify it, you want to eat it. You are now at the sixth level, called **relationship**. You make the connection between the banging of large, shiny objects together and a sharp clanging noise – pulling a long, furry object and barking – hearing distant voices or horn-like noise and seeing people appear – water and a cup.

"What all this means is that, as small children, we are building an understanding of the world from our perceptual signals as we sense our environment. This building process continues throughout life. As I explain the higher levels, you will learn how you create both your perception of Betty – as wife, mother, lover – and, as a consequence, how you decide what things you should or shouldn't do in your relationship with her."

Bob held up his hand. "Hold it. Doesn't Betty influence me?"

"Sure she does, but *it is your interpretation of her actions through your perceptual system that determines how you actually perceive what she does.* It is how you construct this meaning yourself through your perceptual system that makes your own world unique and different from all others.

"Because your brain constructs this meaning, it is unique to you and only you. Also, you are completely unaware of the meaning others are making out of the same environment. I'm sure your wife is perceived quite differently by each of your children, and, yet, it is hard for us to imagine that others haven't constructed things exactly the same as we have. As we get into the higher levels, this difference in how we each perceive people will become clearer.

"Even though all perceptions are subjective, the various levels I have described so far usually produce perceptions that are fairly similar to what others might perceive, primarily because they are still at the experience level. So what we have talked about thus far might be called *common experiences.*"

"It's hard to imagine just having a common experience without it having a name," Bob said.

"That's because you're not a little child. Remember, we have long since passed that stage. Because we were so very young when that happened, remembering how we perceived a world of pure experience without naming things is impossible. At least for me it is.

"These first six levels seem to come from *out there*. We all can see a ball bounce, hear music, taste an apple, feel the touch of soft skin. We observe events and act on the relationships of various events. When we were small children, our brains constructed a model of the world we experienced as detected by our perceptual systems. That was all we knew since all information came through these systems. As we grew older, the higher levels came into play, and you will see that they will *seem to come from within ourselves*. It is at this point that people create perceptions from the same environment in remarkably different ways."

"What do you mean by 'come from within ourselves?' " Bob asked.

"The higher levels involve creating concepts or symbols rather than understanding a physical experience. These higher levels are built exclusively on those six layers of experiential knowledge that have already been developed. It is the variety of personal experiences and how we have chosen to build them into perceptions that are the sole bases upon which our conceptual understandings are created. We are aware only of what our experiences tell us. Thus, our personal judgements and the symbols we create rely on how we have constructed this experiential knowledge, which we've sensed at intensity level from the environment. Symbolically, I can't explain Mexican refried beans even though I've seen them, smelled them, and tasted them – nor can I explain what it is like to be happily married for thirty-eight years. I can think of analogous experiences, but it isn't necessarily the same. I am also sure that you and I will never understand the experience of giving birth to a child," I said smiling.

"You know, this is strange," Bob said, half smiling. "I come in here for counseling for stress and depression, and I end up trying to learn how I think. It certainly isn't what I expected, but there seems to be a definite connection. Now, if I understand you correctly, when I have an opinion of Betty as my wife, it is really that I have created my own unique perception of her. Isn't that what you are saying?"

"You've got it, Bob. And, speaking of unique perceptions, you've just introduced the seventh level which is **category**. Calling Betty your wife puts her into your classification of *wife*."

"What do you mean by my classification?" he asked.

"The word *wife* is a category. With category you may say to yourself, 'There is Betty' and then, at that point, substitute a symbol *wife* for the actual person Betty. From then on, you may only think of Betty in terms of the characteristics that you have created for the concept *wife*. You can get into difficulty when you build the idea of *wife* into your head and then expect your specific wife, in your case Betty, to conform to that category."

"You really hit a raw nerve there," Bob said. "She is always complaining that I expect her to treat me like my mother treated my dad. The other night, I came home late, about nine o'clock, and she was in bed reading. I went into the kitchen, fixed my own meal, and ate in silence. Boy, what a homecoming! My dad was a doctor, and my mother always fixed something for him when he came home."

"How did you deal with Betty?"

"While getting ready for bed, I made the comment that she could have at least sat at the table with me while I ate. She just replied that if I had called her like she wanted me to, then she would have fixed the meal when I got home."

"What is it that you wanted?" I asked.

"I just wanted her to show some affection toward me," Bob said sadly. "I'm out there busting my butt for the family, and my evening at home is to sit silently at the dinner table while the rest of the family is off in their own little world somewhere else in the house. So I take my food into the living room and watch TV while I eat."

"Did your comment to her about not sitting at the table while you ate help you to get what you wanted?"

"No, I guess it didn't," he said, throwing up his hands in disgust. "I see what you mean. Things got worse when I mentioned something about how she was gaining weight and ought to exercise a little."

"What did you want?" I asked.

"I hate living with a fat woman, and she's getting fat," Bob said, showing some disgust. "I keep telling her about gaining weight, and she just keeps getting more upset and fatter. I'd just like to see her lose a little weight, take more pride in herself."

"Do your comments to her about her weight get her to lose weight?"

"Hell, you know the answer to that!" Bob said angrily. "She just keeps getting fatter. I can see her turning into a beach ball with legs if she doesn't stop gaining so much weight."

"Do you think you can control your wife's actions?"

"Obviously, I can't," he said, calmer now with an element of resignation in his voice. "I really do care about her. I just want to be happy with Betty, that's all."

"I'm glad you do. Now, with respect to categories, they are very useful because they allow us to form symbols in order to reason about our experiences. A child begins to use symbols when words begin to identify experiences. An eighteen-month-old baby may point and say 'Daddy' or 'Mummy'. Children say 'Want cookie!' or 'Big dog!' The minute children start to see similarities in experiences from any of the lower levels and start to conceptualize categories, they put a symbolic stamp on what they perceive. For example, children might see something as 'funny' or 'cute' or 'dumb'. They can also categorize actions they perceive through experience at the event level, such as washing a pan, throwing a ball, smiling at a friend, or scratching their back. This is how they form categories.

"As we mature, this can be very confusing because we tend to lose sight of the individual differences that people representing a category may have. When you see Betty as *wife,* it can be your idea of *wife,* and suddenly it is no longer Betty that you are dealing with. If you have some very individual ideas about how wives should act and they are really quite different from what Betty actually does, then how much chance is Betty going to have in your eyes?"

"Not very much," Bob confessed, seeming a little embarrassed. "I guess I don't give her much chance to just be herself. It never occurred to me that I perceive her both as herself and, at the same time, as my idea of *wife.*"

"It's the difference between the intellectual view of the world and just the experience of it. The intellectual view, which is perceived at the five higher levels, deals with just the concept *wife, mother, lover,* and all the other ideas my wife, Hester, represents. My experience with her, which is perceived at the lower levels, involves my day-to-day interactions with her, the things we do with each other, the things we say. To be less aware of one set of levels than the other makes us that much less human and makes us open to all kinds of problems. If we let words push us around and we begin to think only in categories, then we may begin to lose our connections with what we experience, for it is from this continuous daily experience we have with another, or lack of experience, that we form our concepts and develop our perceptions of those about us. My perception of Hester has changed considerably since our marriage thirty-eight years ago, primarily due to the time we've spent alone together. We'll talk more about this when we get to quality time. As far as dealing only in categories, it doesn't allow for much growth in a marriage."

"I see what you mean," Bob said. "I guess the same is true with my children, my boss, my employees, everyone I deal with. I expect them to be a certain way and, when they don't measure up to the way I think they ought to be, I think they've got problems. But really, I'm the one with the problem. There's a lot to learn."

"You'll get there." I smiled as I handed him another sheet of paper.

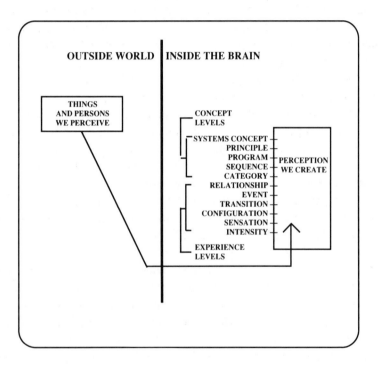

"After category comes the eighth level, which is **sequence**. When I go to bed, I execute a sequence of categories. I take off my clothes, which is a category, take a shower, another category, brush and floss my teeth, open the window, and crawl into bed – all categories. At sequence level, it's the order in which things happen that matters. In the morning, after I wake up, I get out of bed, then I put on my shoes. Those are two categories of actions. If I put on my shoes first, then get out of bed, I would see that as the wrong thing to do. It should be the other way around. Sequence is what makes the difference.

"As we look at the next level after sequence, you will see that a series of actions is again involved, but now the element of conscious decision-making is added. The other day Hester asked me to deliver some posters from her poster gallery to the homes of several customers and then to pick up some materials she needed. As I attempted to work my way through a network of streets, continually making decisions as to which was the most efficient route to follow, trying to find the homes for which I had an address but which didn't seem to be in the logical place, I was executing a **program**, which is the ninth level.

"This is the level where we reason out what to do, where we make a series of decisions in order to achieve something we want as we attempt to deal with the environment. For me, shopping for groceries is the perfect example. I have to decide which fruits are the best buy, then individually check for ripeness. I then check for lowest prices and freshness in the vegetable bins. I'm making decisions throughout the whole operation."

"Do you mean this is where I define what I want?" Bob asked.

"Not exactly, but at program level you construct an understanding of what it means to reason things out and make decisions. When you decided on something, you can only choose from those things which you have experienced. You can't want something you haven't perceived. Wanting Betty is not specific enough. You must have an idea of what you want her for, and some idea of the standards by which you are going to deal with her. But we are getting ahead of ourselves, and this might sound a little confusing."

Bob nodded vigorously. "It does!"

"Hang in there," I said, laughing. "We'll get back to that. At any rate, at program level we begin to understand how we deal with our environment to satisfy our internal wants. As we interact with the world, we become conscious of two things. First, we have some effect on the environment, and this interaction alters our perceptions. Second, in the process of dealing with the world, we find ourselves analyzing our choices. 'If I do this, then what happens?' This is the essence of the program level. We are building an understanding of thoughts and actions, what they are and what they do. We watch others do things, and we sometimes try the actions ourselves – whether drinking beer in our teens or striking up a conversation with a stranger in a gas station. First, however, we build our own unique understanding of our experiences, whether through watching others or through our own interactions with our environment.

"We continually watch others accomplish various tasks, especially our parents in our early years. We see how people interact with their environments to satisfy their goals. We see them make choices."

"That's interesting," Bob said. "It's like my kid watching me fix a flat tire or paint a room. He learns how things are done. He has to perceive it and understand it at the program level first and then he attempts to do it himself when the need arises."

"That's right, although he could also be more creative, and come up with the idea himself or think of an alternative way of accomplishing the same task. But, essentially, you've got the idea.

"At the tenth level, called **principles**, we begin to realize that there are some conditions under which certain actions seem to work and are acceptable and other conditions under which they are not. It is from these experiences that we set standards or guidelines and establish certain rules. I remember when my son, Thomas, was two and I cursed at something that hadn't gone right. The next thing I heard was Thomas using those same words. I realized that I had different principles for swearing when I was alone than when my young children were around. Thomas' swearing was something I didn't want, and I began to re-evaluate my standards for swearing.

"Principles initially evolve out of our many daily experiences of interacting with our surrounding environments. From the business person who has to make decisions affecting employees and customers to the unhappy spouse who is considering an extramarital affair, from the citizen who is filling out an income tax form to the judge about to decide a case in which he holds a very strong prejudice – we all face decisions involving principles. Even deciding what to eat for dinner involves comparing what we eat to a set of standards. When we face a new experience for which we have never established a standard, hopefully we'll do one of two things. We'll either evaluate the values and beliefs that reflect that category of experience, or we'll review the consequences of our actions to determine the needed standard. In this way, we are operating at principles level.

"Initially, we use our past experiences when we determine the standards we set. As a driver, I learn the areas where 'the police are active' and may decide to set my standards accordingly. As a married man, I have learned my wife's tolerance level through experience. I have learned how much abuse my body will take before it 'complains' when it comes to excessive eating or exercise or not enough sleep. I learn the limits to how much abuse people will take. When we get to talking about what we want, you'll see how many standards are set through the interaction of how we build our perceptions and what we want. However, the bottom line for me in dealing with others efficiently and satisfactorily is my set of guidelines based on internally set standards or principles.

"Eventually, a style of living evolves out of the standards I have set – a belief or value system, my own personal culture. As a company man, perhaps you might call this your own corporate culture. This evolving set of beliefs is what I call my **systems concept**, the eleventh level. It is best described as *the way I think things ought to be*. It includes all those values that are important to me."

Bob cocked his head. "That's what you were asking me about earlier, wasn't it?"

"What's that?"

"You asked me what was important to me in my life, and then you asked me to prioritize the items. You were getting me to deal with my systems concept, weren't you?"

"That's right, Bob."

"But there's something I've never understood," Bob said. "My brother, Jim, seems to put his wife and kids first. He and his wife, Harriet, are pretty happy. They're always going places and doing things. Betty and I never do much of anything. But Jim and I had the same parents."

"That's because our parents don't build our unique understanding of the world. We do. We build our own worlds from the material that's available to us, from the environments in which we find ourselves. We may have the same parents, the same teachers, the same extended family and neighborhood friends, but it is how we *perceive* people and what they do that influences how we build our worlds. Think of the enormous variety of experiences we perceive on a daily basis and the number of ways there are to perceive them. A person's actions may be humorous to one, offensive to another, boring to a third, and so on. The critical facts are how we build our own perceptions and the different meanings that are possible for every experience we encounter.

"If I were to ask Betty, each of your children, your boss, your employees, your peers, your brother, your parents, and everyone else in your family to describe you, do you think any of them would describe exactly the same person?"

"Well, no, I guess not," he answered.

"If their perceptions of you are different, how many more differences might there be in their general ideas about marriage? Remember, Bob, that we build our systems concepts only from what we alone have constructed from the environment in which we live. As we construct our ideas of family life, work ethic, friendship, truth, justice, religious concepts, they will be derived from the environments in which we find ourselves and based on the perceptions we create in our own minds.

"My ideas of family life and intimacy reflect my experienced ideas that I have learned from how my father treated my mother, from my own experiences with the many women I encountered in life, from the media, and from the ideas I have imagined after having read about and observed life around me. My systems concept is the foundation from which flows the very center of what I stand for, for what I believe in. Thus, my systems concept is formed by me and is a product of my own individual perceptual development. It's my personal blueprint for happiness."

"They can change, can't they?" Bob asked hopefully.

"Sure they can. My systems concept is constantly changing, depending on how well it serves me when I attempt to build a satisfying life as I deal with my environment. Say that I have a belief that doesn't work for me – when I put it into action, it runs counter to my world and doesn't lead to satisfaction in my life – I have a number of choices. Among them is the option to change my systems concept. Another option is to re-prioritize my values within my systems concept."

"I just never thought of how important my relationship with my wife should be," Bob said, shaking his head. "I guess you never really think of these things until, as you say, you're faced with a crisis that forces you to look at your priorities. But I'm still a little unclear. How do people create their systems concepts?"

"Well, Bob, often we choose the values of others with whom we are close, such as our parents, teachers, friends. However, when the actions of the people we love are contrary to what we perceive as their values, a conflict arises within us concerning whether to continue to accept the value and reject the behavior of the person, or vice versa.

"Remember, children are exposed to our values in a number of ways. They experience how we treat them, they hear what we say, and they watch how we deal with others within and outside the family. They also observe how we apply our moral values. Do we return something that isn't ours, do we make sure we pay what we owe to others, and, in the privacy of our homes, how do we speak and talk about others?

"A further dilemma is presented to children when each of their parents demonstrates a different set of values. One parent may show violence, another total insecurity. One might never insist on setting standards, allowing the children the complete run of the house. Another may vacillate between a strict code of behavior and an I-don't-care-what-you-do' attitude.

"At the systems concept level we construct a cluster of ideas which we believe will lead us to peace and happiness. We create these values for ourselves based on what we have experienced. We develop values from what we perceive within the environments in which we live. Obviously we are attracted to what seems to work for others as well as for ourselves. Also, for a child, the stronger and more enjoyable a relationship with a parent, the more likely that parent's value system will appeal to the youngster. The dilemma occurs when there is no real, warm relationship between parent and child or when there is a conflict between what a child's parent does and says.

Bob looked down at the floor and shook his head. "Then I can see where my kids have probably had a real problem with their father. I haven't been around them very much over the past years and, when I am, it's never really pleasant."

"Our values can be learned from our parents, at least until we test them as we are faced with decisions which bring them into conflict with other values. They could have developed from those life experiences which have seemed to work for us and which we have found sufficiently satisfying. I also think that we have been endowed genetically with a system that has its own unique demands and influences what is satisfying to us. However, that's something I'll talk about later when I get to reorganization."

"So where do we go from here?" Bob asked.

"Well, we've discussed how you build your own unique percep-tions of the world, including your value systems and how you set priorities. Now, let's take a look at standards and see how these relate to the specific things you want to accomplish."

Bob looked me in the eye. "I'm ready."

Chapter 3

EVALUATING VALUES, PRIORITIES, AND STANDARDS

"To help us build our own perceptions of the world, nature has provided us with a storage facility called *memory*. As we observe, experience, and think about our environment, we store in our memories our own created versions of events and then recall them when we have the need. During your development, you constructed your idea of what marriage is supposed to be, and, when you got married, you implemented that concept."

"But I really didn't want the kind of marriage I have," Bob protested.

"I'm sure that's true. You built your world by using your perceptual system. Then you stored what you built in your memory. Anytime your system senses a lack of satisfaction, you draw from your memory those perceptions that seem best to meet your demands. You really can't want anything unless you've created it in your perceptual system and stored it in your memory. You can't want a certain model car unless you are aware of it. Nor can you look forward to eating a mango unless you have already tasted one.

"One problem with not being able to create a satisfactory marriage is that you may not know how to build the kind of marriage you want. That's something we'll talk about later. Another problem – one that many people have – is that you have a lot of other unsatisfied areas of importance that you've wanted to improve. Since you are limited in time and energy, you have been forced to decide that some things were more important than others."

"My priorities," Bob said. "That's why you asked me to examine my priorities."

"That's right, Bob. The lower the priority, the less likely you are to satisfy that desire. Your family was number three on your list, giving it little time. If your boss demanded more work or you felt like going to the gym for your health, your family had to wait until you had first satisfied the other priorities.

"*Everything we do or think must be in harmony with our systems concepts.* The reason I began with what was important to you is because everything we want must first be in harmony within our highest order – our systems concepts. Identifying and assigning priorities to our values is a critical first step in resolving conflict and eliminating stress."

"What do you mean by 'within the highest order?' " Bob asked.

"Well, suppose you wanted to serve humanity as a social worker in a residential treatment center and you also believed you should help your three children through college and into their first homes. Social workers in residential treatment centers are at the lower end of the professional pay scale, and college educations and homes are expensive. Do you see any incompatibility between these two goals?"

"I see what you mean," Bob said, nodding.

"I saw a single parent recently who felt a very strong sense of responsibility about raising her three children and had a similar strong urge toward developing a close, committed relationship with a man. Can you see how we can have two goals that may be incompatible? It's that incompatibility or conflict within our systems that's the cause of our stressful feelings. In the case of the single parent, after evaluating both goals in terms of available time and possible added conflict, she decided to raise her kids alone."

Bob sat forward. "Incompatible goals are something we struggle with at the plant. Everytime we increased production on a certain line, product quality went down. We decided that quality came ahead of cost savings."

"That's why it's best at first to deal with our systems concepts and set our priorities. Everything we decide to do will then be based on our values and beliefs in order of importance. At your plant, product quality is more important than reduced costs. The small amount of time you've spent with Betty and your children was dictated by your belief system and what you thought was important."

"I guess I'm not that great a person, am I?" Bob said sadly, looking down at the carpet.

"Bob, did you intentionally mean to hurt your family?"

"Well, no, I never wanted to hurt them," he responded.

"Did you intentionally try to give your family as little time as possible – wanting to stay away from Betty and ignore your children?"

"Of course not! I just thought what I was doing . . ." Bob stopped short and thought a moment. Then he continued, "I was just following the way I thought things ought to be. I guess I wasn't bad, I just didn't think through and evaluate what was really important to me, and because of that my family suffered, and so did I. Tell me, what do I do now?"

"Bob, do you think it's my job to tell you what to do? Or would you rather that I teach you how to think things through so you can decide how to handle those problems for yourself?"

"If I learn to think things through, I won't need a counselor," Bob said grinning.

"That's right," I said, grinning back, "and we will have successfully accomplished our individual goals, mine to teach you and yours to handle your problems. Now let's get back to looking at the principles level that we talked about earlier. What naturally evolves from what we believe and value are our standards or guidelines, which are at the principle level. Standards are merely our own internal guidelines and criteria for decisions we make. Suppose you have set a standard of eight hours per night for how much sleep you should get. That standard would be your guideline for making a decision at the program level for when you should go to bed."

"I see that all the time at work," Bob said. "My department sets the standards which serve as a guide for the decisions of those people who make our products. Come to think of it, we have a company policy book which we hand out to all company employees. It spells out all the rules and regulations for the entire work force."

"Whether we consciously think about it or not, we have standards for every belief system we have. The problem is that we rarely have spelled out these standards even to ourselves and have almost never evaluated their effectiveness. Thus, our actions which flow from our standards operate randomly at best. To function effectively as persons, we have to examine our beliefs and values, create and articulate effective standards and then use them to guide us when we have to make decisions at program level. Real problems occur when we are faced with a dilemma and we haven't really set forth any standards. Can you imagine how much internal turmoil we are inviting for ourselves? Sometimes not setting standards is at the heart of a problem."

"What do you mean?" Bob asked.

"Here's an example. A fifty-five-year-old man recently came to see me who was twice divorced and had been dating a woman for nearly a year. She failed to show up for a date one Saturday night. She called the following day and said that she had met a former boyfriend and had spent the weekend with him at a resort. This naturally upset my client, and he wondered whether he really wanted to continue this relationship, even though he had grown quite fond of her.

"Let's call them Wayne and Susan," I said, wanting to keep their identities confidential. "Wayne is a wealthy man, highly successful in a large corporation. He had been uncomfortable being sexually involved outside of marriage. Susan had always been completely honest with him, and she assured him that her relationship with her former boyfriend was completely platonic. My client was unnerved and at a loss as to which direction to take. During the several weeks prior to seeing me, he had dated several other women, but he missed Susan. He had grown quite fond of her during their ten-month courtship.

"When someone has a problem concerning whether or not to become involved with another person – whether taking on a new partner in business or in a romantic relationship – the solution often does more harm than good, especially when choosing one person over another."

"What do you mean?" Bob asked.

"Well, let me explain. Most people compare one person's personality to another's, rather than measuring it against an objective standard that flows from their own internal standards."

"Run that past me again," Bob requested.

"Let me show you what I did with Wayne. Then I think this will be clearer. Rather than talk about the pros and cons of Susan, I asked him to list his standards for the kind of woman he would like for his wife, forgetting for the moment about Susan or anyone else.

"He said he had tried this prior to marrying Esther, his second wife. That marriage had lasted less than a year and had ended in a disaster. He said he had been looking for a woman who professed the same faith as he did because his first wife never went to church. He didn't want anyone with young children; he'd already raised a family. He wanted a non-smoker like himself. Finally, someone who really liked sex. He said he thought that he'd found her, especially someone who liked sex, but he never was told it would be over once they got married. As he put it, the glacier moved in.

"At any rate, Wayne's list certainly hadn't worked for him. He needed a more comprehensive list, one that involved his intended spouse's total personality, one that would be compatible with his own. In short, *it had to flow from his systems concept level — namely, his values.* He began to list his standards. He thought that honesty was vital to any relationship, especially in marriage. He also believed his future wife should have a successful career of her own, and that they should also have compatible interests and careers. Moral standards were important as well as having similar cultures. Finally he suggested that his spouse should be attractive to him and that she should be fun.

"I suggested several more standards for his consideration. I do this only after clients have given their own ideas so as not to influence their choices. I just try to suggest ideas from my own experience in an area where my clients may not be familiar. Wayne liked my suggestion that the potential spouse had experienced a warm, healthy, long-lasting, non-sexual relationship with someone of the opposite sex, especially with a parent or sibling. That kind of experience helps us construct an appreciation of the opposite sex as having a strong, worthwhile value."

"That's rather tough on those of us who come from disrupted or broken homes," Bob said, with a note of concern.

"You're right, Bob. It really isn't fair, but I believe those who have experienced this kind of relationship tend to have more respect and see more value in the opposite sex. When there is early sexual involvement and a lack of a healthy, close friendship with the opposite sex, people are less likely to perceive their partners as someone with value. When you commit yourself to loving someone, the less value you see in that person, the less likely you are to keep that commitment. Committing yourself to a stranger is nowhere near as binding as a commitment to someone for whom you have a deep respect. In Wayne's case, he would be looking for a woman who already had formed a perception of what a close friendship was like without being involved with the compromising aspects of sex. After marriage, the intensity of sex is eventually diminished, and it becomes a normal aspect of intimate, marital love. Not having this understanding of genuine love can lead to real problems later on, namely, not knowing what's needed to build the kind of intimacy for which we are all striving. Thus, those who have had a prior understanding of a healthy, non-sexual friendship are more likely to perceive their intended spouse primarily as a close friend, and not just as a sexual partner."

"Well, I know many people who have lived in really disrupted homes and yet seem to be stable," Bob protested. "Besides, how many warm, loving homes are there these days?"

"Bob, I didn't say only in family life. I said especially within a family. A person getting married is literally creating a family with another person. There's a lot of give-and-take in family life that's rarely found anywhere else. Remember that your control system is designed in series, and the first six levels are pure experience. You construct your idea of a spouse through that experience and attach a symbol to it at category level. It is that healthy, intimate, long-term, give-and-take kind of relationship you have created that goes to make up what you call *spouse*. It's a very unique concept, not at all like that with a close friend you see occasionally. I might add to my list a close relative that took the time to care, but that would depend whether you lived long enough with that person to establish the kind of experience that would reflect what I'm trying to define."

"How about a teacher or a counselor?"

"I don't think it's the same thing," I replied. "We only see these people occasionally, we don't live with them. Without that intimate, day-to-day living, I don't think it is the same."

"I guess it does make sense, now that you've explained it a little more," Bob said, "and I can see how it's hard to find a substitute for a close, family relationship. I can also see how it would make a difference in how couples would get along."

"Another area that is critical to me is that the person be uncon-flicted. This is best demonstrated in a person that has no debilitating habits, such as an addiction to alcohol, drugs, food, gambling, and things such as these. I would also exclude people who are easily depressed, get angry quickly, appear highly insecure, are very self-critical or critical of others, or exhibit a lot of anxiety – in short, those who show difficulty in dealing responsibly with their own problems. Any of these behaviors is easily identified when a person is faced with a conflict, especially one having to do with relationships.

"At any rate, Wayne came up with eleven items. Then, and only then, did I ask him to list them in order of importance."

"Why not just have him state his priorities as he was giving them to you?" Bob asked.

"I didn't want him to be judgmental while thinking creatively of his standards or criteria. Anytime you have creative thinking going on, it's counterproductive to to be judgmental of whatever is said. Setting priorities only after all the standards have been listed allows each standard to be given equal consideration. Once Wayne had listed his standards in order of importance, I asked him to list the women he might be considering. He listed Susan. Then he added Dotty, his first wife, who had since remarried, then divorced and had recently begun making overtures to him. Then came Terry, an attractive business woman he had recently begun to date. Then Bridget, a woman his attorney had introduced to him. Finally, his second wife, Esther, in whom he had no interest but wanted on the list anyway.

"Considering Wayne's financial background, it was no surprise that he decided to use numbers from one to ten in deciding how each woman measured up to his own internal standards. He added that more consideration would be given to those who measured favorably to his highest prioritized standards. This is how Wayne's standards looked after he had set the values." I handed Bob the list 'Wayne' had allowed me to share with others as long as I protected everyone's anonymity.

Wayne's List

	Susan	Dotty	Terry	Bridget	Esther
1. Unconflicted	3	4	8	4	0
2. Honest	10	0	8	5	2
3. Compatibility	0	3	7	7	6
4. Prior relationship	0	6	6	7	3
5. Successful career	2	0	10	7	0
6. Attractive	8	6	10	6	10
7. Fun	9	4	10	6	10
8. Moral standards	4	4	7	5	0
9. Similar culture	6	6	7	0	4
Total	42	33	73	47	35

"The important thing to remember is that he was comparing what he wanted in his future spouse with the various women in his life. He was not comparing one person with the other, an approach which can be very disastrous."

"Why?" Bob asked. "I have to choose a new foreman at work. How else can you select someone?"

"Well, Bob, when you chose a woman to be your wife, her total personality has to be as compatible as possible with your own value system, namely your systems concept. This can only be evaluated as you extract from your values those standards for *wife* which you want her personality to reflect. Comparing one person to another rather than to those standards doesn't reflect what is important to you, but rather how two or more women compare to one another. Also, when you compare one person to another, you eliminate a possible choice – neither one."

"So what did Wayne decide to do?" Bob asked.

"He decided not to decide. He wanted to let a little more time pass, to relax, and date others, especially Terry."

Bob raised one finger. "O.K. When it comes to choosing a foreman, I should first decide in my own mind what qualities reflect my own internal world, my systems concept, then set standards that reflect those values. Then I should look for a person that fits those standards rather than compare the various candidates against each other. You know, that makes a lot of sense, and it deals with a problem I have at work. However, I'm already married, not choosing someone new."

"Standards apply not only for ourselves, but also whenever we deal with others," I suggested. "They aren't just for choosing someone, but for dealing with people and situations that already are part of our lives. It could be a case of choosing someone to marry, or working out a way to get along with an existing partner in business or a spouse, setting criteria for one's own self, or selecting an employee or a school to attend. The more our standards reflect our own internal worlds, namely our systems concepts, the more our choices will be consistent with what we want and the easier it will be to live with that choice in the future.

"Because others we work or live with have their own internal control systems just as we do, it is critical that whenever we have to interact with someone, especially on a regular basis, the standards by which we interact always have to be agreed upon. I have a close friend who set up a business partnership with a friend and the friend turned out to be very ineffective. Because there was no agreed upon termination clause, it cost my friend a lot of money to buy his friend out and take over the business himself. He could have saved himself a bundle of money by having set standards ahead of time."

"You know, I was just thinking," Bob said. "I'd like to get my daughter, June, in to see you. She has this guy she's been going with, and I have an idea, if only she would first reflect on her standards for the kind of man she wants to marry, she might give him up."

"I'd be glad to see her, Bob. I just had a sixteen-year-old girl in here yesterday. She was going with a twenty-eight-old-man, and her parents were literally crawling up the walls. She's a junior at a local high school and has a B average. I got her to look at her standards for the man she would want as a husband. She came up with eight and added three of those I suggested for a total of eleven. Then I asked her how her boyfriend compared to the list she had made. On a scale of one to ten, he only made it above five with one standard. After she did the comparing, she looked at me and said, 'Do you think I'd better find another boyfriend?' I just said, 'That's up to you.' "

"That sounds like June's problem. Her mother and I have been trying to talk to her about Charlie and what she has been doing to herself. The guy quit college in his freshman year and hasn't held a job for more than three months. They've been living together, and I've been paying her part of the bills. There are times when I think I'm half supporting this creep too. The whole thing is a mess. I've talked to her until I'm blue in the face."

"What have you been saying to her?"

"Well, I've been telling her she shouldn't be just living with this guy, that it's wrong," Bob replied. "I can't understand that girl. She used to be so normal. She worked hard at school, had good grades, ran around with a nice group of kids, had boyfriends but nothing serious, you know, no fooling around. Then she gets to college, and she changes completely. I can't understand it."

"I guess she's changed her systems concept and her standards," I suggested. "Or perhaps she's testing out those she has learned from you."

"Why should she want to change her standards?" Bob asked. "Betty and I have been teaching her those standards since the day she was born."

"Maybe she sees that they haven't been working very well for you and Betty," I said softly.

"What do you mean?" Bob said, showing some concern.

"Well, have your values and standards brought you a happy marriage and a warm family life?"

"Well, no, I guess not," Bob said, looking down dejectedly. "I've tried. God knows I've tried. I guess I'm just human, that's all."

"And to what race does your daughter belong?" I asked.

Ignoring my comment, Bob continued, "My parents were divorced when I was sixteen, but I still held on to their values. I tried to follow those values. I just don't understand. How do standards develop for those who come from unhappy homes?"

"If we grow up in an environment with one or more people who we believe really care about us, then we tend to accept the things they do because the results of their actions are pleasing to our own internal system and compatible with our goals. As we begin to gradually form our own standards and values, we tend to make these values our own.

"As we reach our pre-teens and develop more social awareness of others, we are faced with dealing with people whose values and standards differ from our own, so we begin to test our ideas. If we find that our internal belief system runs counter to every attempt at making friends, then we begin to look at alternative systems to satisfy our goals."

I rummaged through a stack of papers, extracted a *USA Today* article, and handed it to Bob. "I clipped this a few years ago. What's the date?"

Bob read, "October 21, 1986."

"Right. This educational psychologist at UCLA, Rod Skager, did a survey of 7,500 California seventh-, ninth-, and eleventh-graders on their use of alcohol and drugs. He found that seventy percent had been high on either alcohol or drugs by age sixteen. However, thirty percent were very resistant to getting drunk or trying illegal drugs. Their major reason for steering clear involved internal values and personal identity. Those kids were saying, 'That's not the kind of person I want to be.' School drug education was shrugged off as ineffective. The kids had made their decisions based on their values – not from what others said.

"Trying to talk people into accepting standards that aren't compatible with their own values and goals or trying to get people to do what they don't want to do never has worked well and never will. It's important that you understand how these three highest levels interrelate." I handed Bob another piece of paper.

How The Highest Levels Interrelate

Systems Concept – values, the way we believe things ought to be

from which evolve our

Principle – standards, criteria, or guidelines

on which we base our

Program – decisions, the things we decide to do

"When a person is faced with a decision about what to do in life, which is at the program level, that decision has to be compatible with the personal value system and the subsequent standards, otherwise there is going to be internal conflict. When you tell people what's right or wrong, when you push them into doing things, when you continually offer advice – unless they want your input, you are forcing them to choose between their desire to hold on to their relationship with you or to do what they want to do. This can create all kinds of havoc within a human control system. We will talk more about that later."

"So you're saying we build our value systems from what's given us the most satisfaction in life, what's worked for us," Bob said.

"That's correct, Bob. We can change those values and standards, and we do so quite often. We do so when, as I mentioned earlier with young teenagers, we try to satisfy our goals based on our present values and things don't seem to work out for us. A couple in their 20's may be experiencing a miserable marriage and have a value system that excludes divorce as a solution. Ultimately, if they aren't reconciled, they may re-evaluate their stand on divorce."

Bob sighed. "When Betty and I first met and even through our courtship, we got along so well together. We were so happy. Soon after we were married, our children came along, and things started going down hill. It didn't make sense because our standards hadn't changed."

"When we begin the process of courtship, we have already established a primary want for involvement with another person. We have established within our systems concepts and principles level a whole set of values and standards which apply to that particular time and setting. There is a certain sexual awareness and excitement unique to that time in our life, and the newness with someone in whom we see value and who sees value in us encourages a greater intensity.

"We also have built within our systems a perception of that person, which may be accurate or not, but which is unique to that time. We tend to ignore those qualities which might otherwise concern us and ignore the thought that we are going to have to deal with these things later. We tend to 'give in' and to 'overlook' many things. We spend hours with that person. We purposely build an illusion of joy which may not really have much basis in fact. Our values and the standards that apply during that time are just for that time. It is not that we are deceitful or bad or stupid. We just want to build an intimate, loving relationship with another person, and we make certain adjustments to what would be our

normal interaction with another. We create an inaccurate perception
and then, unfortunately, we act upon it.

*"Once we have gotten a committed relationship, then our view of
our partner can really change. We no longer see that person as
someone we want, but rather as a spouse, someone we have.* At the
same time, the excitement of the physical intimacy with someone new
is no longer there, and, hopefully, an enjoyable routine has taken its
place. Sex no longer holds center stage, but takes its rightful place
within the marriage. Sometimes there is disagreement on what that
rightful place should be.

"What can be a disaster is that the married partner, who, during
courtship, held center stage, now is relegated to third or fourth spot
within our systems concepts. The values and standards for how we live
with our spouse are not the same as those for our lover. Same person,
different criteria. And with a change in our standards comes a change
in how we treat our former lover, now spouse. In short, we become a
'different' person. It is not that we want to destroy our marriages or hurt
our partners. More positive values have, no doubt, always been there.
It is only when the intended partner becomes an actual partner that we
shift to a different set of standards, which, in actuality, also have always
been within our systems. In other words, a lover may be number one
priority in our systems concepts, and a spouse number three. Same
person, different priorities. As our perception shifts from lover to
spouse, our values and standards shift as well to reflect the new
designation. For the most part, few people recognize this happening."

"Good Lord!" Bob exclaimed. "I never knew that was happening."

"It happens all the time. New employees generally work quite hard
as long as they perceive themselves as being on probation. Once they
become regular employees, protected by all kinds of laws or labor
contracts, there is a change in how they perceive themselves, thus a
change in which values and standards apply, and often subsequent and
sometimes obvious changes in their output."

"What you are saying is that we behave according to how we
perceive ourselves," Bob said.

"And others," I said.

"What do you mean?" Bob said.

"Your wife is one example," I suggested. "Just think of all the
significant people with whom you interact every day and see how
differently you act around them. How do you perceive your boss?"

"As a workaholic and unappreciative," Bob said.

"Did you always perceive him that way?"

"Well, no," Bob said. "When I first began working at the plant, he was manufacturing manager, and I liked him."

"Do you treat him differently now than you did then?"

"Well, yes, but he's different," Bob said. There was a long silence and then he added, "You're right, Ed, he really hasn't changed that much. I guess I perceive him differently now that I work for him instead of with him."

"Would your standards and subsequent actions be the same with a person you liked as they would be with a person you saw as a workaholic and unappreciative?"

"So, it isn't my boss that's the problem," Bob said thoughtfully. "It is how I perceive him. I guess that's what you were trying to point out when you asked me how I perceived Betty. Then how do you change a perception of someone who keeps belittling you?"

"What do you have control over, Bob?"

"Myself," he answered.

"In light of what we have been talking about, where do you think you could begin to deal more effectively with Betty, with your boss, and with others?"

"I guess I have to look at my values and standards with relation to my wife," he answered, his voice lowering. "I'm still a little confused."

"Bob, let me use an example. Recently I had a young woman come to see me who had been suffering all kinds of stress in her life. Call her Joan. Joan is a nurse, a recovering alcoholic, was not too close with her family, lived alone, smoked, and had only one friend whom she saw very little. On her third visit to see me, she was my first appointment, and I was late. She had been shown into my office. During her prior visits, we had discussed these ideas of reviewing values, setting priorities, and so forth. When I arrived, she had listed her values, the standards for achieving those values, and decisions she had made based on those standards. I was so impressed I asked if she would allow me to use her list as an example to others who are interested in developing these ideas for themselves. Here's her list."

I handed Bob a sheet of paper, and he studied it thoughtfully for a few minutes.

Joan's List

Values	Standards	Plan of Action
spirituality	attend AA meetings	2-4 meetings/week
	meditation	10 min in AM
		10 min before bed
	work with sponsor	talk 10 min. daily
	read basic AA text	read 15 min. at lunch
	work 12-step program	do what sponsor says
health	regular exercise	use ski glider-3x/wk
		exercise grp-3x/wk
	eat well	vegetarian diet
	practice hygiene	wash hair, self daily
	see counselor	see Ed 1/2 hr per wk
professional	follow work rules	arrive 15 min early
		growth review charts
	show others respect	compliment others
		smile at patients
		follow orders
	professional growth	med. reports at breaks
close family	quality time w/mom	walk with mom 3x/wk
	contact sisters	visit sister 1x/wk
		call other sister
close friends	involve with groups	join hiking club
		volunteer work 1x/wk
	individual friends	Amy quality time
		3x/wk

Bob looked over Joan's list, how she had set her standards, and her plan of action for each set of standards. Finally, he looked up and said, "I'd like to use standards to help myself."

"Well," I said smiling, "let's take your priorities one at a time, and see what standards might guide you in making decisions as to how to act. Ultimately, at program level, you are going to have to make decisions as to what plan of action is best for you. However, in order to make decisions that are compatible with the higher orders in your entire system, you should first review and evaluate your systems concept regarding women in general. Then review the concepts of wife, lover, and mother of your children in particular. Set these values in order of importance to you. Finally, you set standards or criteria to guide you in making decisions about how you will deal with Betty. You can then use the same process in dealing with others as well."

"So how do I begin?" he asked, leaning forward.

Chapter 4

RESOLVING THE FIRST OF MANY CONFLICTS

"Bob, what is your idea of 'Woman'?" I asked, tracing quotation marks in the air with two fingers of each hand.

"I don't know. I've never even thought of 'Woman' as an idea before." Bob mimicked my gesture. "What do you mean?"

"Well, except for the obvious physical differences, do you see women as an essential part of your life – socially and professionally?"

"I guess, when it comes to work, I'd rather not have to deal with too many of them," he admitted ruefully. "They seem more aggressive than men and not as easy to kid with. You know, you have to be careful you don't say something offensive, things like that. They're too emotional. Don't get me wrong, Ed, I'm not against them working – equal rights and that stuff. I'm just more comfortable dealing with men.

"As far as my marriage goes, I see Betty more as a partner, both of us trying to do our best to make ends meet and to get along. What with the expenses of raising kids today, she and I both have to work. She's my wife, we live together although we aren't very close. I usually can't talk to her like when we were first married. We should be getting along better, that's for sure."

"Do you see her as someone you would like to be closer with, more intimate?"

"I'd like to get along with her better," he answered, "but I've never been real close with anyone before – except for my dad. Well, there is Tom, a friend I had in high school. We were real close, did everything together. He's still around, and we play golf at least once a week. We're still good friends."

"So you never saw a woman as someone you'd like to be really close with, is that right?"

"Yeah, I guess so," Bob said thoughtfully. "I'm attracted to women, you know, but they're different and I feel more comfortable with Tom. We understand each other and can talk. It never has been easy to talk with women. They have different ways."

"So your idea of 'Woman' is someone with whom you'd like to raise a family and get along with but not necessarily be intimate friends. You find it uncomfortable interacting with women at work on a regular basis, regardless of whether she's your supervisor, peer, or subordinate. Does that sum up your idea of 'Woman'?"

"I guess so," Bob said, somewhat concerned. "I really don't want you to get the wrong idea. It's not that I mind working with them, I'm just uncomfortable having to deal with them too often. That sounds really bad, doesn't it?"

"I'm not trying to be critical of you, Bob. What you have said is neither good nor bad. It's just the way you have built your idea of women in your head, within your systems concept, and this influences all the standards you have set for dealing with women and all your actions that flow from those standards, whether at work or at home."

"It's just how I've always thought about them," he said defensively.

"Let's take a look at the standards you've set that guide how you deal with women. Do any women supervisors work for you?"

"Yes, Julie is head of personnel and training, and Beth is the finishing line supervisor," he replied.

"Would you say that you had different standards for dealing with Julie and Beth than for dealing with the men who are supervisors?"

"Well, sure, I don't play golf with them," Bob replied.

"Do you play golf with all the men?"

"No, just certain guys."

"Do you have any specific standards that lead you to restrict your activities with Julie and Beth but not with the men?"

"I'm very careful how I go over production problems with Beth so she doesn't think I'm criticizing her," Bob said. "I also praise her when quality is high, and I don't do that on any of the production lines. It's funny, I never thought about doing those things until you asked me how I work differently with Beth."

"How about Julie, do you treat her the same as other supervisors?"

"Julie's my boss's ear," Bob said. "She takes everything that's going on in the plant back to the boss, so everyone stays clear of her. I avoid her as much as possible. She brings in these training programs that are a complete waste of time. Everyone avoids her whenever possible. I probably am able to avoid her more than the rest though." Bob grinned, then continued, "Everytime she asks me to come to her office, I make sure I have something else to do so she has to come looking for me."

"So you do deal with her differently than you do other supervisors."

"I guess so," Bob said, his smile gone.

"Do you see any connection between how you perceive women and the standards you set for dealing with Beth and Julie?"

"I guess if I perceived them as more equal, my life at the plant would be easier, especially the way I treat Julie," Bob said. "She's so typical of a woman."

"Did you hear what you just said, Bob?"

"I see what you mean," he said, sighing. "I guess I am slightly prejudiced. I look at Julie as a typical woman, and I don't want to have to deal with her."

"Do you see how your perception of women influences your standards in dealing with women?" I asked and then added, "And these two in particular?"

Bob paused. "I never thought of it like that before."

"Let's take a look at the standards you've set for dealing with Betty. How about money, how are decisions made when it comes to making purchases?"

"Well, we've really never had much of a problem with money until recently," Bob told me. "Anytime we needed something we just went out and bought it. We always did have our own accounts. Lately, I've been paying bills that Betty generally takes care of, like the department store credit cards. I just don't know what she's doing with all her money. She makes a good salary."

"Do you ever discuss important things with her, such as your job, the children, large purchases, or the personal problems you're having?"

"No, I can't talk to her any more," Bob said, a note of anger in his voice. "She won't listen, and when she does bother to listen, she starts correcting or criticizing everything I say or do. When I protest, she gets mad. As far as discussing job problems with her, she wouldn't be interested. As far as personal problems, I talk those over with Tom. Tom is easy to talk to."

"Would you be talking to her about anything in particular if the two of you were getting along?"

"Like I told you, we used to make all the major appliance purchase together, although I always bought the cars," Bob said. "But her last car she purchased herself. She didn't even tell me she was going to buy another car."

"What is the standard you have for spending time with Betty? This would include the important things you consider doing with her and the amount of time you two should share alone together each day?"

"We used to eat dinner together every night, but lately she's been attending a lot of evening meetings. We watch television sometimes, but she likes to go to bed early and read. Lately, by the time I get to bed, she's asleep. Doesn't sound all that great, but that's how it is."

"Bob, earlier you said you wanted a happy marriage, to be close to Betty, isn't that right?"

"Well, yes, I really do," he said, with frustration in his voice. "I'm not sure how to be close to her. Hell, Ed, I'm not even sure what close is anymore."

"Do you see any connection between how you perceive women, your idea of a wife, the standards you have set based on those ideas, the actions that flow from those standards as related to your present unhappiness in your marriage?"

"Well, I just never thought about any of this stuff before," he said, shaking his head. He paused a moment, then added, "Yeah, I'm beginning to see a connection. I never saw much wrong with the way I perceived women, but what you're saying is that if I'm not doing too well around them, then I had better check out how I perceive them."

"You're right on track, Bob! We're able to judge the validity of how we have built and organized our entire perceptual systems, especially the levels where we deal with concepts, by the ease with which we interact with the environment, including the people around us. In other words, if we're satisfied with the way our lives are going, then our systems concepts, our standards, and those actions that flow from our standards must all be in harmony with one another. The opposite is also true. When we're not satisfied with the way our lives are going, it means we have to re-evaluate our systems, and re-set priorities or reorganize our systems concepts or values, our standards or guidelines, and the decisions we make. We've just looked at your view of 'Woman'. We could also spend time with your ideas of marriage, children, work – all kinds of areas. In the long run, they all influence the satisfaction in your life."

"Even if I could change the way I view women, it's pretty hard to change the habits of a lifetime. And she'll be the same as she is now."

"Bob, do you remember my talking about the program level?" I asked. He nodded. "At this level, we not only make a decision to do something, but we make choices along the way. For example, suppose

I decide I want to spend time with Hester after she gets home from her poster gallery. I decide to start getting dinner ready to save us time in the kitchen. Suppose that half way through preparing the meal, I decide to put on music and then bury the garbage in the garden. I might find the garden needs watering and take on that project next, which is something she usually does in the early evening. Then I might decide to return to the kitchen, fix a salad, and set the table. All of these are choice points in the general program of wanting to spend time with Hester during the evening.

"Now, as human beings, we tend to eliminate making choices, especially where repeated acts are involved, by forming habits. This helps us accomplish things more efficiently. We recognize these unconscious patterned actions or thoughts, which occur in series, as evolving from prior conscious choices. As a baby, once you have learned all the muscle coordinations necessary to feed yourself with a spoon, your system programs that function in. Ultimately, we just decide to eat, and our patterned actions take over. Starting a car involves a variety of decisions which, when made over a period of time, are reduced to the one initial decision of deciding to start the car. Imagine all the conscious choices driving to work on your first day for a new company. After several weeks on the job, you have discontinued many of the choices you made at program level, and they are now only perceived as part of your habit for driving to work.

"So habits are formed through a series of conscious decisions at various choice points based on something we want to accomplish. These actions are repeated over a period of time until we're making fewer conscious choices to accomplish the same task," Bob said thoughtfully. "But then how do you help people get out of their habits? Some are almost impossible to break."

"You do it by asking people to evaluate their actions at the place where they would logically make choices if they had been operating at the program level," I replied.

Bob suddenly smiled and said, "Now I understand why you were asking me whether the way I was talking to Betty was helping me get what I wanted."

I smiled back and nodded my head. "That's right. I was trying to get you to evaluate a habit pattern you had created in the past and that you were using without really thinking through what you were doing. At program level, I was asking you to re-evaluate all the various things you were doing that had become a habit.

"When people come to me for counseling, much of what they do is habitual. Over the years, they've developed styles of dealing with others that are highly ineffective – but those styles have also become habits. They've done them so often that they no longer make conscious choices, but have developed a patterned way of dealing with others, about which they have little or no awareness. In short, they've formed a habit.

"Remember the demonstration with the rubber band?" I asked. Bob nodded. "What caused your actions to change?"

"Wanting to keep the knot over the dot and watching the relationship of the knot to the dot to make sure the task was being accomplished," Bob replied. "I don't get the connection."

"Remember how you were unaware of the movements of your hand, that you were concentrating on watching the knot in relation to the dot?" I asked. "Your hand movements represent your actions, what most people call behavior. Watching the knot in relation to the dot is merely your perceptual system feeding back into your brain the results of your actions. Without that feedback, your system wouldn't know whether it was accomplishing its goal. The critical issue here is that you're primarily conscious of only two things – what you want and the results of what you're doing. I call these **feedback**."

"Yes, I remember that, especially the example you gave of the cruise control," Bob responded. "You said we really don't think of how hard we press on the accelerator, which is our action, but rather the result of our action, namely the reading on the speedometer."

"Exactly. All of our actions are designed by us. We decide the specifics of what we do at program level, such as how hard we press to hold a cup, the location of our lips and the angle of a cup when we take a drink, or how easily we place a cup on a table without spilling its contents. Very young children struggle to learn these behavioral skills which we have long since acquired.

"The real key is that once these muscle coordinations are learned, we no longer think of the specific action. We just decide at program level to take a drink from a glass and then sense the results, how it tastes, which is what we wanted in the first place. How we picked up the glass, the angle at which it was held, its weight – all of this is automatically done by a system that we have designed to accomplish this task, which uses our feedback system to compare with what we want."

"So all we do is consciously decide on something and then consciously watch ourselves get what we want. Is that right?" Bob asked.

"It's not always conscious. We are generally aware of getting the thing we want most, and many sub-tasks get done without our thinking about what we're doing. Have you ever eaten a meal with a friend and suddenly realized you had eaten the piece of bread you were about to butter or had an empty glass from which you were about to take a drink. Your main concern was your conversation and the interaction with your friend, so your system – having already been designed to accomplish the job of eating and drinking – just went right ahead and took care of those tasks. Our systems operate as efficiently as possible. These are what you called earlier 'the habits of a lifetime.' Remember, not only have we taught our muscles how to deal with what our nervous systems want, but we also operate in a similar way at all levels of our control systems. For example, we develop ideas at category level of what we see as delicious food, an enjoyable game, or a sport that's fun to watch. These new ideas are added to our memories and become an integral part of how we view the world. Because there is nothing biological to tell you that your perception of the world is quite different from other people, you begin to believe that the world is the way you perceive it. Then you run headlong into the reality of other perceptual systems, whose owners believe their world is the way things really are, and you find their ideas quite different from the way you perceive things.

"Suppose you invite me over for what you believe to be an enjoyable meal – spareribs, only to find out that I'm a very strict vegetarian. You ask me out for a game of golf, and I suggest a long, fast-paced walk instead. Finally, you suggest watching a pro basketball game, when you find that the only sport I really enjoy is pro football.

"As habits are formed, we take the same route to work, even though traffic is backed up. We find ourselves at the soda machine, without having consciously decided to go there. We respond in the same automatic way to our bosses or peers, depending on how we perceive them at that time and what we want.

"The way we enter our homes, how we respond to our spouses, to each child, to the dog or cat, to the neighbor – all has to do with what is presently the most important thing on our minds, how it's ranked in relation to other items of consequence, and how we perceive the persons or things we are dealing with. Once our wants are decided, our perceptions formed, and various choice points have long since been made at program level, then our patterned actions take over."

"You know, I see where I do that with people," Bob said. "The other day, one of my foremen asked me why I always criticize something he's doing before I say anything else. I didn't realize I did that. I suppose I developed that way of dealing with him and have always used it, without being too much aware of what I'm doing. I never thought that we just watch the results of what we are doing. The result I was watching wasn't how he dealt with me, but the quality and on-time delivery of his product."

"That is the problem of forming patterned habits. We only are conscious of the feedback from the entire sequence of events, not from the individual category of each event which makes up that sequence. When you're having difficulty with someone, it's best to move what you want and have been doing sequentially to program level, where you will be making evaluations and choices all along the way."

"What do you mean?" Bob asked.

"Let me ask you, what is it that was uppermost in your mind as you approached the foreman?"

"Well, I was worried about quality control on the assembly line."

"How did you deal with the foreman?"

"I criticized his results and then tried to pep-talk him into doing better," Bob replied.

"Is the way you're dealing with your foreman getting you what you want?"

"No, I suppose it isn't. The quality of his work hasn't improved at all. I guess I need to look at how I'm dealing with my people at work."

"That's what I mean by making evaluations and choices at program level. What you were doing is dealing with the foreman out of habit. In other words, you developed the habit of dealing with others when there are problems by criticizing and then pep-talking. Do you see how the only time you become conscious of what you actually said is when I ask you to evaluate the relationship between what you wanted, which was better quality control on the line, and what you actually perceived yourself doing, criticizing and then pep-talking your foreman. Internally, our system is continually comparing what it wants with how it perceives inputs at all levels, but it's at program level where we have to consciously learn to evaluate whether our present actions are helping us achieve what we want. What all this means is that when you've got problems, you better move to the level where problems can be resolved. In this case I moved you to program level."

"Yeah, I see what you mean," he said, adding, "At least I think I do."

"Remember, our decisions at program level are guided by our standards, which are based on our values. It's logical that when we've got problems making decisions, we have to review not only how we want things to be but also our guidelines or standards, because our standards are based on our values. The prejudice that many hold against women and various minorities is generally found at their systems concepts level. All their standards and actions flow from these biased beliefs. When there is prejudice against a woman, you'll see it when she enters an all-male department. The standards for her will be different and probably a lot more difficult."

"I guess I'm as guilty as anyone," Bob said. "When Beth was being considered for foreman, I remember checking her work in her previous job pretty carefully. I guess I was holding her to greater accountability than the two men who were also being considered. She's turned out to be one of the two best supervisors I have. So I really have to define and re-evaluate what I want, and change how I perceive things if my life is going to get better?"

"That's right, Bob. We can do this examining what we want at systems concept level by setting standards to guide our actions, by deciding what actions to take at program level, and by testing those ideas by imagining how things might work out. We then come up with what we imagine to be the best of all alternatives to accomplish what we want. This is called plan making, and this act of thinking things out is called **internal feedback.** That's because we imagine the results in our mind.

"Once we decide on a course of action, we try it out and see how closely the results match what we wanted. This is called **external feedback**, because, instead of imagining what might happen as we did in plan making, we actually experience what does happen and compare the result, the feedback, with what we wanted. Here's a diagram adding feedback to what we've talked about." I handed Bob a sheet of paper.

"That's easy enough to understand," Bob said. "At the plant, sometimes the quality control team works out a better plan for testing the product, which is what you would call internal feedback. Then we try out the testing equipment on the production line and see how it measures up to what we wanted, and that you call external feedback."

"You've got it."

"Only one thing puzzles me," Bob said. "I came in here stressed out, and you're getting me to deal with my family life and my job. Is that what's causing my stress?"

"Bob, most people define stress in terms of its physiological symptoms such as high blood pressure, stomach upset, stiff necks, back

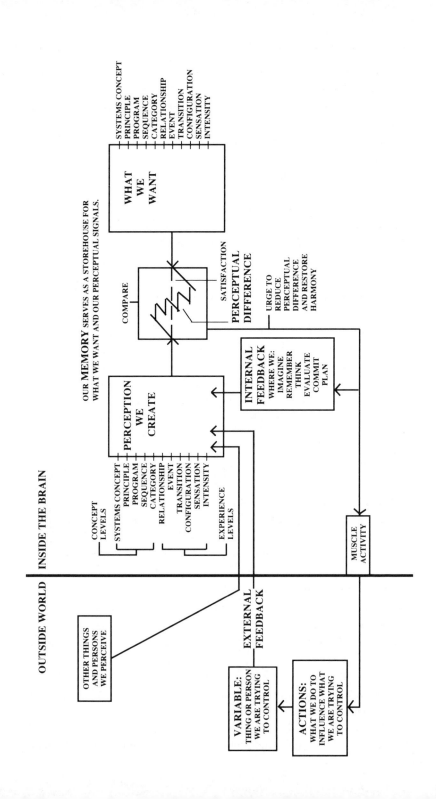

pain, headaches, inability to sleep, and feelings of anxiety, irritability, anger, depression, and tension. These symptoms are real, and most treatment is attempted through discussion of the past, expressing present feelings, various relaxation exercises or prescribed medicine, none of which get to the real causes. These methods deal solely with symptoms.

"How stress really works in our systems is something we're dealing with now, through learning how your system works. As I further explain all of this in subsequent meetings with you, these ideas will become clearer. To answer your question briefly, any time you have internal disharmony within the various levels of your system – and it's chronic – you will suffer the kind of discomfort which is felt as stress. That's why I'm having you examine those things that are important to you, the standards that reflect your beliefs, and the decisions you've made. Your judgement was that a major area of conflict in your life was your relationship with Betty, so we are dealing with that first, that's all."

"I see," Bob said.

"Are you ready to work on a plan for improving your marriage, or do you want to deal with another area in your life?" I asked. "You seem to be more concerned about your problems at work."

"No, I want to work at my marriage, I really do," Bob said emphatically. "I suppose I really do put work first, but I want to change that. I truly do!"

"Earlier you said that you've had a close relationship with two people, your dad and Tom, but that intimacy with a woman, in a way similar to your relationship with Tom, was not something you perceived as desirable. Are you still comfortable with this idea?"

Bob shifted around in his chair, thought for a moment, and then said, "Before you asked me my idea of 'Woman' and about being close, I hadn't really thought about the idea of being closer to Betty – just about getting along. I guess it would be kind of better, you know, a close friendship. It just sounds a little strange to me. As I said, I've never really thought of it before."

"Is there much physical affection between you?"

Bob shifted some more, looked down at the floor, then admitted, "No, not very much. We don't have sex very much, about once or twice a month, and when we do, she doesn't seem too anxious. She used to kiss me when I left the house and came home from work, but she doesn't even bother very much with that lately. To tell you the truth, there hasn't been much of anything in the past year or so."

"We talked about the standards you have for spending time with her, and you said that the little time you have spent recently has been in front of the television. You even said she was generally asleep by the time you get to bed. Is there really anything besides watching television that you two do together?"

"Well, not really. When we do go out, it's always with another couple, generally friends of hers from the bank or people from the club. It's O.K., I guess, but we don't do things alone together. It seems I'm alone even when we're together. Doesn't sound so great, does it?"

"Do you really want to work at the marriage?" I asked, trying to make sure he was fully committed.

"Yes, I do," Bob said. "I'm just not happy at all. I'm miserable. I want to be closer with Betty."

"Is what you're presently doing with Betty helping you get what you want?"

"No, of course it's not," Bob snapped.

"And you really want to work at this?"

"Yes, I really do," Bob said, looking at me and nodding.

"O.K., then what's your plan?"

"I have no idea what to do," he said. "You tell me! I'm a good engineer, and I do a pretty fair job of running the plant, but I'm not too great when it comes to women, that's pretty obvious."

"Well, engineer's set standards for how a product is to be manufactured so that the end product meets certain specifications, is that right?"

"That's right," Bob replied.

"The same thing happens when you want to improve a relationship. You have to set standards for how often you should interact, what you're going to do, and who's going to be involved in the activity. Right now, the only time you spend with Betty is when you watch television together. Are you satisfied with what you're doing when you're spending that time?"

"Well, it's all right, I guess," Bob said.

"If your friend, Tom, wanted to just sit and watch television instead of play golf, would you be satisfied with that?"

"I get your point. Maybe I could get Betty to take up golf."

"Imagine that you had moved in with Tom for three months, how would you spend evenings with him?"

"Well, we like to play gin rummy and scrabble," Bob said, smiling. "And Tom likes to take walks. He hates riding the golf carts, says it's for lazy people."

"Now, compare that to how you're spending time with your wife. Do you see how differently you look at the time you want to spend with Tom compared with how you've been spending time with Betty?"

"Why the difference?" Bob asked.

"You perceive them differently. Your perception of Tom is of someone with whom you want to continue maintaining a close, intimate friendship. Your perception of Betty is someone with whom you want to maintain a working relationship, but, from what you've said, you've never thought of her as someone with whom you really want to be close. It's how we perceive people in terms of the categories in which we place them and what we want that determines our actions.

"You've placed Betty in the category of *wife,* and you perceived *wife* as someone with whom you're supposed to get along, but that's not a close or intimate relationship. You've perceived Tom as a close friend, which carries with it the concept of intimacy for you, and you've maintained that close friendship over the years. The standards you set and the actions that flowed from those standards are what you've been living. With Tom, it has been very satisfying for you. With Betty, according to you, it's been a disaster.

"Remember, Bob, your idea of the symbol or word *friendship* is based on the experience of friendships you have had in your life. All those things you've done with Tom go into that idea, as well as any other close friendships you've enjoyed over the years. Betty you perceive as *wife.* Your experiential concept of wife was formed primarily by the marriage of your parents. After twenty years of being married to Betty, that same concept of *wife* is still determining the way you relate to her. What you need to do now is to create a whole new concept of *wife,* which is analogous to your category of *close friend.* So what do you think?

"I guess I'd better start spending the kind of time with Betty that I do with Tom," Bob replied, shaking his head.

"The kind of time you spend with Tom I call quality time. I've spent the last twenty years developing criteria for quality time."

Bob looked puzzled. "Why does quality time work?"

"By spending this kind of time with your wife, you will be able to construct a new meaning for *wife.*" Bob still looked confused so I continued. "You see, the reason quality time works is that we construct perceptions of people based upon how we have experienced them. Most couples spend their free time together passively watching television or a movie. Quality time activities involve creating the enjoyment while maintaining awareness of our partners. Also, there has to be a mutual commitment toward the goal, whether it's recreational or the completion of a necessary task, both of which are generally perceived by most as enjoyable and fulfilling. We tend to tie our perceptions of the experience to the person with whom it's shared since our partners are an integral part of the activity. If you are really committed to building a warm and loving perception of Betty and you regularly engage in these kinds of activities with her, creating a caring perception of her will become much easier. However, you must have a strong commitment. If you work at this relationship and you don't have a strong commitment, the marriage will fall apart."

"Why is that?" Bob asked.

"As you begin to sense a closer intimacy through quality time, it will test your sincerity with respect to how much you want the marriage to work. If you really don't want the marriage, the increased sense of closeness will become more repugnant to you, and you will quit working at the relationship. If both of you are committed, then you will start to grow closer, and the marriage will begin to improve."

"I guess if I want to think of Betty with the same warmth as I do Tom, then I'll have to set the same kind of standards, and we'll have to do the same kinds of things I've been doing with him. Maybe Betty and I could start taking walks in the evening. What do you think?"

"Do you think it will make things worse?"

"Are you kidding?" Bob asked, laughing a little. "Things couldn't be much worse than they are."

"So, if your standards are to spend some kind of active time with Betty through quality time, then you have to work out the particulars before you start. Here is my quality time card which details the specific kinds of activities that build a strong and lasting marriage."

Bob took the card and read it over. Finally he said, "Everything on the left side under number one is what Tom and I have been doing. We even spend that time alone – just the two of us – and we do it every week. On the other hand, Betty and I don't do anything together. Nothing. I know this works, cause it's worked for years with Tom and me."

He was quiet for a moment, and his eyes began to moisten. Then he added, "I wonder if things would have been different had I spent more time with my kids and less time with Tom. I guess my priorities really are screwed up. Tom is a real good friend, but I placed him ahead of my own children. That's what I've been doing all along. Oh God, what a mess!"

LOVE/QUALITY TIME

based on perceptual control theory - by Edward E. Ford

LOVE - Willingness to spend quality time every day alone with another no matter how your partner behaves and without trying to control the other person.

CRITERIA FOR QUALITY TIME

1. DO ACTIVITIES THAT PROMOTE AWARENESS OF EACH OTHER AND CREATE PLEASURE THROUGH MUTUAL EFFORT.

such as:	not:
playing games	watching TV
exercising together	going to the movies
working in a business or at home	just being together
doing projects or hobbies	taking a drive
dancing one-on-one	listening to music
taking a walk or a bike ride	watching others

2. DO YOUR QUALITY TIME ACTIVITIES ALONE TOGETHER, NOT WITH OTHERS.

3. DO YOUR ACTIVITIES ON A REGULAR BASIS.
   A minimum goal should be at least 30 to 40 minutes per day, five to six days a week.

To guarantee a close intimacy, both must be totally committed to spending quality time alone together on a regular basis. To make sure quality time becomes a habit, create a graph (see other side). Also, make a written list of what you actually do during quality time and how much time you spend doing each activity. Both the graph and the list should be kept for at least a month.

QUALITY TIME ILLUSIONS
— eating together — talking together — having sex
These activities do not create strong relationships,
they can only enhance a love that already exists.

QUALITY TIME ENEMIES
— talking about the negative past — extremely self-critical
— individual problems — very controlling or critical of each other
— spouse is intimately involved with a third party
— using a person, a past event, or how you feel as an excuse

"Bob, do you want to go over this card with me?" I asked quietly.
"Yes, although it's pretty clear, at least in terms of the kinds of activities. I can understand what you mean when you stress the importance of a commitment. Keeping track of what I'm doing goes back to what you said about building a new habit. That makes sense."

"Under illusions of quality time, I mention how talking doesn't build a relationship. Again, understanding control theory, when you're talking with someone, whether you're eating or not, you're interacting at the symbol or category level, exchanging concepts. You need to experience Betty as a person on a regular basis if you want to influence how you perceive her. We build our ideas of love through the experiences we have with others, but we've already gone over that."

"I can understand why sex is not a vehicle to building quality time," Bob said. "When we were getting along, it was great. We both enjoyed it. Now, it's only for physical relief, and it offers little of that."

"The enemies of quality time reflect those things that just make things worse – things that tend to drag the marriage down."

"I can see that from what you've written here," Bob said. "I like this card, it makes sense. I've just got to get going on it."

"When is the best time for both of you to spend this time, and when and how are you going to ask her to spend this time?"

"Will you talk to her?" Bob asked. "I'll tell her to come in."

"Bob, does she know you're here?"

"No, I haven't told anyone I was coming here," he said, a little embarrassed.

"Do you think it a good idea to tell her to come in?" I asked.

"No, I guess not," he said dejectedly. "How should I handle it? I don't want to blow it."

"Let me tell you what seems to have worked best for other clients who come in without their partner. The best thing is to tell the truth. Tell your wife that you went to a counselor, that you were all stressed out, and that your main concern was your relationship with her. Then ask her if she wants to work at the relationship with you."

"What if she says that she doesn't?" Bob asked, sounding worried.

"You might ask her if she would be willing to work at it for a few weeks, which lessens the commitment," I suggested. "At least you will have tried."

"If she says yes, should I ask her to come in?" Bob asked.

"No, that is something that has to come from within her. What might happen is that she may ask you what you want her to do. Your response should be, 'That's up to you. I went in for help, and he's helping me. If you want to go in and see him, that's fine, and if you just want to work at the marriage by spending more time with me, that's fine too. It's up to you what you want to do.' That way, you're respecting her own internal goals and are not trying to control her. The less you try to control people, the less damage you do. We'll talk about that the next time we meet. So, what do you think? Does the plan make sense?"

"Yes, it's fine," he said grinning. "I like it!"

"Are you willing to do it?"

"I sure am," he said.

"So, tell me what are you going to do?" I asked, wanting to make sure Bob had in mind a plan that spelled out clearly how he was going to deal with his wife.

"Well, I'm going to tell Betty that I have gone for help, that I'm all stressed out from my problems both at home and work, and that, as a beginning, I would like to work on our marriage," Bob said. "Then I'm going to ask her if she will work with me on our marriage, that you have given me some ideas that might make it better. If she's willing to work at the marriage, then I'll suggest going for a walk or playing cards or scrabble. If she refuses to work at the marriage, then I'll call for help." Bob laughed after his last remark.

"That's great, Bob! Would you call me after you've had your talk with Betty and let me know how things went. Assuming she wants to work at it, I'll see you next week at the same time. Otherwise, I may want to see you earlier."

"That's fine by me," Bob said, smiling. "I feel a bit better already."

Bob called that evening. He said that Betty admitted she too was unhappy and had asked Bob if she had to see me as well. Fortunately, Bob told her that it was up to her – that I had helped him. Betty called me the next morning, and we set up an appointment for the following afternoon.

Chapter 5

DEALING WITH FEELINGS

Betty appeared at my office door at precisely the time we had set the previous day. "Betty, I'm glad to see you." I smiled as we shook hands. "Thank you, Ed. It's nice to meet you," she said, somewhat formally. She sat down, posture erect.

"How can I help you?"

"I don't know what Bob has told you," she began. "This may be hopeless. I've been married to him for twenty-four years. We were married right out of college. He'd gotten his masters in engineering, and I had my undergraduate degree in business finance. We had two children right away, and then, a few years later, I started working for a finance company. Then Tim came along, and I took off work again. When Tim was two years old, I got a job with National Bank. I took a leave of absence for a year when I had Ruthie.

"I have spent all these years working hard and raising a family, and I have nothing but loneliness to show for it." Tears welled up in her eyes. "I'm so frustrated and angry, I just want to walk away from it all. I have a husband who spends his life on the golf course or in front of the television, a son that's an alcoholic, another son that's spoiled rotten, and no one that really cares about me." Betty paused, trying to blink back her tears.

"The one thing that I have is my job. I'm branch manager for National Bank. I've been with them for thirteen years. Except for the usual problems that women supervisors encounter these days – condescending remarks and a few employees with whom I'm having some difficulty – I'm reasonably satisfied with my job, and I'm treated fairly well. Sometimes I feel like taking Ruthie and leaving Bob with the mess. She's the one ray of sunshine in our family.

"Bob just doesn't care about any of us. When he gets upset, which now seems like a daily occurrence, he just goes into his shell. He won't talk to me. He never has. Lately he's been doing a lot of criticizing. When I try to get out of him what is wrong, he just shuts down. He says I don't listen, but I do. This is all so crazy. When we were first married, I tried to live with his usual style of dealing with problems by avoiding them, but I'm just so sick and tired of being ignored. I feel so angry I could scream. I should have left him years ago." Betty's tears were spilling down her cheeks by now.

"Yes, I can see you're upset," I said, knowing that she needed to calm down before I could deal with what she wanted. "How can I help you?" I asked softly.

"Last night he said he wanted to work on the marriage," she said. "I've heard that before. He talked about playing some stupid card game or taking a walk. We've got real problems, and he wants to play games. He hasn't the foggiest notion how I feel. I'm angry and frustrated, and he thinks it can be solved by taking a walk. I try to express my feelings, and he just walks away – holes up like he doesn't care. I don't mean a damn thing to him! I'm so angry, I just can't stand being at home."

"You'd like to get rid of your anger and feel better. Is that what you want, Betty?"

"Yes, I guess so," she said with a little relief in her voice. "I shouldn't get upset, but I'm so frustrated. I've got twenty-four years invested in him, but now I wonder if I've wasted all that time."

"You find yourself angry and frustrated most of the time at home, is that right?"

"Yes, and now I'm beginning to feel frustrated at work as well."

"What do you want to talk about first, your problems at work or at home?"

"Home, by all means!" she answered. "I just don't see how you can help me. I've spent the last six months talking with a counselor, and not one damn thing has changed."

"Then it's your home life you want to improve?"

"Yes, it is," she responded.

"Betty, can you identify the things that you want to happen at home that you perceive aren't happening – the things that are causing you to feel the way you do?"

"What did you say?" she asked, looking a little puzzled.

"In your home life, what is it you want that you don't perceive you're getting and that cause you to feel angry and frustrated?"

"I want a husband that loves me. I want to be able to be intimate with him. I want to be able to tell him how I feel and what I think about things and know he really wants to hear it. I want children who seem to know what they're doing and that I know are doing well," she said quietly.

"That's fair enough. Do you want to work first at trying to improve your marriage, or do you want to work at your relationship with your children?"

"Well, I guess with Bob. I want to work on my anger and frustration."

"You want to work on your feelings of anger and frustration, is that so, Betty?"

"Well, yes, it is," she said, visibly calmer.

"And you said that, in essence, your inability to relate happily with Bob was a partial cause of your anger and frustration, did you not?"

"Yes, I guess I did, but I never thought of dealing with my marriage as a way of reducing the pain of anger and frustration. Somehow you turned things around. I'm a little confused. I've always thought that expressing one's anger is the best way to get rid of it. You're not supposed to bottle up your feelings, are you?"

"Has talking about your anger in the past really helped you?"

"Well, I have always felt better when I express my anger over what Bob or one of the children has been doing. I seem to calm down a lot."

"Does the anger return?"

"Well, yes, when they do something again the anger returns," Betty responded. "I get mad again, especially when it's the same thing over and over and over."

"Then has expressing your anger helped you?"

"It seems to help in the short run," Betty said thoughtfully. "I always thought that expressing how you feel sort of clears the air, makes things better, and helps people understand how they feel. Gets things out. Isn't that true?"

"Has it been true for you?"

"Well, around the house, I express my anger a lot, although no one really cares how I feel." She paused, then continued, "I guess maybe it really doesn't help."

"Do you know how your husband or your children feel?"

"No, I don't suppose I do. They don't tell me. They shut me out."

"When you express your feelings to your family, what are you expecting from them?"

"I guess I'm expecting them to appreciate me a little more and to realize that what they're doing is upsetting me."

"Has expressing your feelings gotten you what you want?"

"Well, no, not really. Oh, sometimes they say they're sorry, but nothing seems to change. They continue doing the same things. It's as if what I said had no real effect on what they were doing."

"So letting family members know how you feel really isn't an effective way of working out problems you're having with them?"

"Well, I never really sat down and thought all this through. I suppose, to some extent, it hasn't been effective. But, then, how else do you work things out except by expressing your feelings? I always thought when feelings are expressed you feel better. From what you're saying, it doesn't seem to solve any problem."

"Has it been really worth it to you to vent your feelings, or does venting your feelings sink you further into the frustration you're dealing with?"

"Well, I do feel a momentary relief, but then I usually feel kind of guilty afterward," she admitted. "I feel badly, and the family is more upset. I don't know. I'm just confused."

"Would you be interested in learning how feelings work in the brain, what causes them, and how to better deal with them?"

"At this point, you've got me curious. I came in here upset and angry, and, right now, I feel a lot calmer. Yes, I would be interested."

"Anytime we want something, that want is actually a patterned electro-chemical charge originating from the various levels of control in our brain. That charge sends out two signals, the first of which activates various motor muscles so we can accomplish what we want.

"The second signal has to do with how we feel. It provides the energy to accomplish what we want by activating the biochemical control systems in our organs that control the emission of hormones, enzymes, and other chemicals. What comes out of these organs are things like adrenaline, blood sugar, and many other substances related to the body's energy management system. These chemicals give us the strength to accomplish what we want and are sensed by our perceptual system at the sensation level as a feeling. Experientially, we identify these feelings at configuration level as a specific feeling. At category level, we label these feelings stress, anger, joy, and so forth. Here's a diagram of what I'm talking about." I handed Betty a sheet of paper.

Betty studied the diagram for a minute. "I saw the diagrams you gave Bob. I had some questions about them." Betty and I discussed her questions, and I outlined to her the ideas on control theory that Bob and I had discussed.

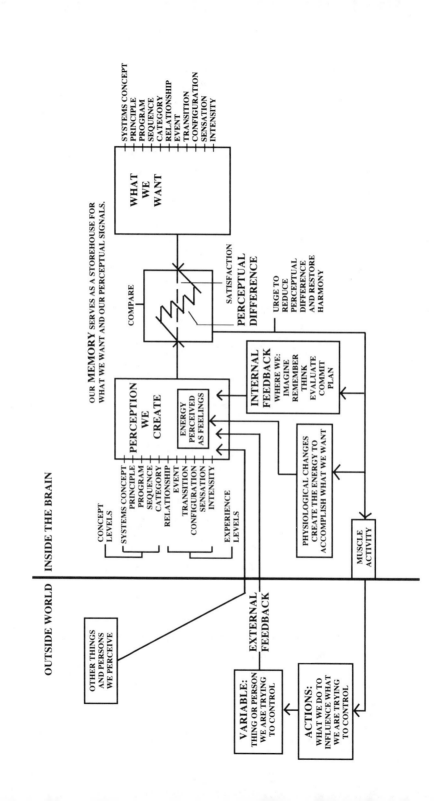

Then Betty said, "This new diagram adds some things."

"Right. It adds the element of feeling."

Betty asked, "Is there ever a time when talking about feelings will help?"

"Talking about how you feel can be helpful when others who have been experiencing the same problem express a similar feeling. This recognition of a similar experience gives you a common bond through which you can identify with others. It gives you a sense of being a part of others, and you no longer feel isolated and alone. This is one of the values of belonging to a group of people with similar concerns. We'll talk about groups later. For now, you still have to work out your problems through dealing with what you want.

"Say, for example, that I want to enjoy my wife, Hester, by playing gin rummy in the evening. She willingly accepts my offer to play cards and we do so. Then what I want is accomplished through what I do. As a result, I feel happiness, joy, or another good feeling. If, on the other hand, Hester decides to retire for the evening, and I persist in wanting her to play cards at that moment, then I will feel disappointment, anger, frustration, or another unpleasant feeling, depending on how I perceive the situation."

"So it all comes back to what I want, is that what you're saying?" Betty asked.

"That's partially true, Betty. First, it's what we want. Second, it's how strongly we want it. When we increase our desire for something, it's represented in our brain by a larger, more intense electro-chemical signal. This, in turn, creates a larger amount of energy which is sensed as more intense feelings, called emotions. The reason people become very emotional about things is that they have very strong desires for whatever it is that they want."

Betty looked puzzled. "I felt that way when I entered your office, yet why did I calm down so quickly?"

"The greater the desire, the more intense the emotion," I responded. "You appeared very tense and upset when you walked in here with what seemed little hope of relief. As you began to realize there was a possibility for some kind of help, the **difference** between what you wanted – peace and happiness – and what you perceived – total disaster – became less, and you sensed a reduction in pain. The stress from your conflicts wasn't relieved, but at least you sensed the possibility of relief. Anytime there is a reduction in pain, it's perceived as pleasure."

"What do you mean *pleasure*?" Betty asked.

"It's like getting novocaine for a sore tooth. Going from the pain of the tooth to the numbness produced by the drug gives a sense of relief which is perceived as a good feeling. Novocaine, by itself, isn't something we'd want under normal conditions. When we're using it for a painful tooth, we want it because it's perceived as relief. Anytime you go from a lot of pain to less pain, it's always perceived as feeling better."

"I see what you mean. But, concerning emotions, I have a friend that cries at the drop of a hat. She's very emotional. I have another friend who always seems very calm, never lets anything bother her. Why the difference?"

"It might have to do with how people have learned to deal with problems over the years. Some have learned to look at the positive side of things or to think about other things when emotionally charged events occur. Others just have learned to cry as a way of trying to reduce the pain of whatever they're dealing with.

"Perhaps another factor may be the third element that contributes to how we feel. As I mentioned, the first element is the specific thing we want, and the second is how badly we want it. The third element involves our perceptions – how we perceive ourselves and others, how we perceive what we are presently trying to deal with, how successful we are in getting what we want, and, finally, the feedback, which is the result of our effort and how well it matches what we want. All these play a pivotal role in how we feel.

"I have had a number of people come to me whose perception of themselves was very critical. This, in itself, often causes a lot of painful feelings. People obviously want to perceive themselves as having value, and, yet, many continually look at only the bad things they do and rarely, if ever, give themselves credit for what they do well. They also look at the bad things that happen to others and that others do. Thus, they lock themselves into chronic misery their entire lives. Are you critical of yourself, Betty?"

"Very!" Betty stared straight at me.

"Have you ever kept a diary?"

"I started keeping one when I was fourteen years old. I stopped when I was about twenty-eight, but I still have them hidden in a back shelf of my closet. No one knows about them, not even Bob. I would die if anyone ever found them."

"Did you ever write good things about yourself?"

"Not very often, I guess."

"Do you think being critical of yourself might have gotten you into the habit of being critical of others. Could it even have interfered with your chances of being close to Bob?"

"I never considered that before. I am, at times, critical of him and the children." Betty paused. "To tell the truth, I guess I do it quite often. On my last performance appraisal at work, that was the one thing that concerned my supervisor. I guess I'm just naturally a critical person."

"Do you think it's natural, or something you learned to do – something you built into the way you perceive yourself and others?"

"If it isn't natural, then why do I do it? I don't want to be that way, and yet I am."

"Well, Betty, recalling the whole perceptual system and how it works in our brains, the program level is where we make decisions that go into the way we design our various actions. We form the style and the way we deal with others from the ideas that occur to us and from how we see others. We especially watch those with whom we live to see how they deal with their environments. Obviously, we start to construct our own style at a very early age.

"Once our system learns all the muscle coordination demanded of a patterned action, it programs that series of muscle movements into memory, and the desire to accomplish something involving that action triggers the whole operation without our conscious awareness of each specific movement.. We don't think through and decide each detail of the way to feed ourselves every time we eat. We've already done that years earlier at program level. For the sake of efficiency, our system always operates at the lowest level, using the least amount of decisions. We have already established the design of the operation through a series of choices. If the program of action is something we use and repeat over and over again, then it obviously develops a stronger predominance in our memory. Eating is something we do quite often. So, when we are hungry, and, because we've already pre-designed our system to deal with eating properly at the table, we enjoy our meal without thinking through all those little actions that are proper.

"This way of simplifying our physical movements is also true of the way we develop thought patterns, our way of perceiving things and setting goals. The more you criticize yourself and others as a way of trying to achieve what you want, the more criticism becomes a part of the way your system deals with it's environment. In short, you've developed the habit of being critical.

"We tend to imitate the actions of those from whom we are trying to learn effective ways of living. Highly critical people have often learned from those who themselves were highly critical. It's hard to build confidence in ourselves when surrounded by those who have no confidence in us, but, if that's the only environment we have, then our options when learning ideas are limited unless we creatively come up with an alternative."

"That was my mother and dad," Betty said sadly. "My dad criticized my mom a lot, and they both were very critical of all of us as children."

"Ultimately, like all habits that we build into our brains – from the simple finger movements to the highly complex way of dealing with people or thinking through problems – these self-critical habits of the way we perceive ourselves are stored in our memories and are called into use when we are facing conflict. Obviously, if the conflict in question involves an area in which I have not done well in the past, such as the area of building relationships, then the response I've designed at program level in my attempt to succeed is going to be to discourage myself. Based on my low self-esteem, all my memories attached to that lack of confidence are going to be recalled. Memories of the past then confirm present actions.

"When people run into some kind of failure, they develop patterns of dealing with others at program level. Then, as a pattern becomes more repetitious, it becomes a habit. People construct their own ways of doing things. Some have designed themselves to say, 'I'll work this out.' Others say, 'I knew I couldn't do it. I'll probably never make it in this area.' The former grow in self-confidence, the latter do not. Self-critical people have a strong tendency to revert to the past, using prior events or past relationships as an excuse for not being able to deal with the present. This can be devastating."

"Why's that?" Betty asked.

"All they have is the accumulation of their past experiences, including past events and relationships, and none of those can be changed. Thus, self-critical people exacerbate the problem by constantly reflecting on their own past failures, increasing the strength of the memories of the events, thus blowing out of proportion what really happened. They paralyze themselves in misery by constantly reflecting on their negative pasts. Therefore, they remain unhappy."

"Doesn't it help to understand why we are the way we are?"

"Of course it does, but the question is whether that's really the reason you are the way you are. Certainly, we can learn to be critical from a critical parent. We also are more apt to learn to handle tension by yelling and screaming if our parents handled it that way. Remember, although the people around us may demonstrate certain styles of living that we may find ineffective in our own attempts to build our lives, we can still build that particular style into our own worlds. Our parents may create the environments from which we draw our ideas, but most people recognize that children from the same family often grow up to be quite different from one another. The way our parents act is no excuse for what we do.

"Everything we have experienced stays in our memories," I continued. "One problem with talking about the past is that it tends to reinforce the memory of the past event, increasing its importance in our minds way out of proportion to the events themselves. Remember, others have gone through the same thing we have experienced, and they have dealt with it differently. So, is it the experience – or is it *the way we deal with it,* both at the time it occurs and in the future, that ultimately determines how we deal with our lives after the experience?

"People who have gone through very traumatic experiences often feel very much alone and honestly believe that no one knows what they have gone through. Knowing that others have had the same experience and, more importantly, learning how others have rebuilt their lives is a big help in recovery. This is the major value of being part of a group of people who have suffered through similar experiences.

"When we go through the trauma of a violent act, such as a beating or rape, because the memory of this event lies only in our brain, there is nothing to tell us from experience that there are others who have also had the same thing happen to them. We feel very much alone and isolated because we believe our suffering is unique to us. Attending a group that offers support and learning that others have had similar experiences helps to alleviate this loneliness, especially for those people who are looking for help on how to build effective, happy lives.

"The real issue in any type of group is that the members talk about how they have dealt successfully with their lives. To sit and cry and moan about how awful it was or is, how miserable it feels, and how unfair it was locks them further into the misery. It's critical that a group deals mostly with how its members have been able to handle successfully the painful parts of their lives – past and present – and, more important, relate the specifics of how they have rebuilt their lives. Each person is helped by learning the positive things that others have done. With group support and the example and encouragement of older members, new participants learn to make individual plans to succeed.

This isn't only true with those suffering from violent fits of anger and severe depression, but especially with those dealing with an addiction.

"The Alcoholics Anonymous program is a prime example of this kind of help. Their meetings provide two benefits – the support system which helps each member identify with others struggling with the same problem and, second, constant reminders from the testimony of others that successful recovery is possible. The most important part of the process is the twelve step program and the insistence on the need for reliance on a power greater than ourselves, which most define as God."

Thinking of her son, Betty said, "I thought alcoholism was a disease, that they weren't responsible for their condition."

"Addicted people are fully responsible for what they do. The difference between alcoholics and most people is that the alcohol works differently within their systems than it does in others. I can control how much I drink, alcoholics cannot. But we all have control over choosing to have the first drink. For the alcoholic or any other substance abuser, it's an obsession of the mind that says 'I can do it.' It's a physical craving that takes over after the first drink, which is when, alcoholics teach, they become powerless to control how much alcohol they consume. It's that simple. That feeling of no power is what is known as the disease of alcoholism. As one friend of mine suggests, alcoholism is a physical allergy coupled with a mental obsession. After that first drink, alcoholics are right back where they started when they quit drinking. This is true of any addiction."

"What about marijuana?" Betty asked. "Mike used to claim that it relaxed him, that it was harmless."

"Marijuana often gives the illusion of eliminating outside distractions and allowing us to focus on our own inner thoughts and feelings. The problem is that the thoughts that flow into the mind are evaluated by a distorted system – distorted by the drug. This creates the illusion of profound thoughts. Current research shows that marijuana is very harmful to the system.

"The real key to all this, no matter what our problems are, is that we can change the way we are. We are not irreversibly conditioned by the past, although we construct our perceptions from the environments in which we have lived. Also, drugs and alcohol won't help us because they distort our perceptions, and, what is worse, they destroy the very systems that they're supposed to help.

"Control theory is the underlying basis for my way of helping people. If it's taught me anything, it's that we're all the captains of our own ships. The hardest thing to learn from this theory is that we should concentrate on our perceptions and wants and not so heavily on our actions. Actions take care of themselves. They're the unconscious patterns that we have built into our brains to help us accomplish more efficiently what we want. They haven't been put there by someone else's behavior as we were maturing. We ourselves build the particular ways we deal with the world. No other person, no one thing, and no one experience caused it."

"What you're saying is in direct conflict with what other counselors have told me," Betty said with a puzzled look. "I still don't understand. If I'm such a critical person, why was I so successful at school and presently at my job?"

"Sometimes we limit our criticism to one area of our lives, such as relationships with people, while we build confidence in our abilities in other areas, such as at school or on the job. It all depends how we have built our perceptions of ourselves as we grow and develop. Besides, a while ago you mentioned how your supervisor is aware of your tendency to be critical of others. That, of course, is the part of your job which has to do with relationships."

"Can you really help a person change the habits of a life time? Lately, I've done a little reading in this area, and most articles imply that past events along with early childhood experiences greatly influence and sometimes cause what we do."

"Most behavioral psychologists deal at the event level," I explained. "They watch the individual actions of their subjects, looking for laws that string them together. They believe that something outside of us causes our actions. Since they don't look within the person, they fail to discern the step by step process of the person's control system at work. Thus, they're unaware of our continuing attempt to maintain a balance between what we want and the results of what we do. It's the struggle to maintain this balance that is the main reason control theory makes so much sense to me.

"The greatest benefit of this theory is that, through understanding it, people can learn how to change their internal patterns. Whether or not they learn really depends on how unsatisfied they are with their present lives and how committed they are to change. If a person has a strong signal within the brain that represents a desire for happiness, and if this person wants to reestablish harmony among the various levels within the brain, that really is the key. Once there's a commitment to learning, then I can help."

"Are you sure you can help anyone?" Betty asked with a smile.

"Well, Betty, not really. I try my best. Anyone with an addiction needs a good program, such as AA. That is the best alternative. I've had little success with con artists and those with highly deviant sexual patterns. The con artist and the loner have one thing in common – they seem to have never had a warm, loving relationship. Unlike loners, who live isolated lives, con artists purposely involve themselves with other people to get what they want. However, their involvement with others seems more of a means to an end than a genuine attempt to establish an honest relationship.

"Let me explain. There are certain rituals, or ways of acting, that are common to those who have made close friendships and who have developed warm family ties. Smiles, handshakes, hugs, ways of expressing oneself verbally, of taking an interest in what others are saying, of doing little things to please others, of going out of the way to be thoughtful. We tend to become very trusting and open when we see these actions in others because we assume that those behaving in this way must have developed the same values and standards that we have through having had warm, trusting relationships. In short, we believe that certain actions reflect specific standards and values.

"Con artists have learned that ingratiating actions, when perceived by others, create a climate of openness and trust. They take advantage of our vulnerability by using these techniques. Their actions are manipulative and reflect their own values and standards which have as their basis the use of others for their own advantage. We interpret these actions as genuine and sincere, but we are fooled. Because we judge the actions to be trustworthy, we trust the person and, thus, become vulnerable to being manipulated.

"Loners will often admit their lack of a close relationship and are often willing to seek help. The con artists see their problems not as truly relational but, rather, as having difficulty satisfying the desires of their own distorted value systems and standards. They have manipulated their own thinking to get what they want, and they value others only as means to their ends. Such a view is so foreign to what satisfying relationships are all about that, for them, real happiness with another is probably impossible. As one young woman with a physically abusive husband told me, 'But, Ed, he can be so sweet and loving when he wants to be, and I just know it's my fault when he gets angry. I just don't want to hurt him. I just don't know what to do!' – a typical remark by a con artist's spouse.

"With regard to those who pursue highly deviant sexual behavior, I believe that they're so focused on the pleasure from their sexual conduct that they're left with little sense of the values of others. The more we see people as sexual objects, the more their worth diminishes.

"This attitude also has a corresponding effect on how we perceive ourselves. If I see you as nothing but a sexual object, then how I see myself will more than likely be reduced in time to that of just a sexual object as well. As I continue to try to find satisfaction within the limitations which sexual intimacy imposes, I will soon start looking for more and more alternatives in the sexual arena to find satisfaction. This search for novelty is going to lead me more and more into the abyss of self-gratification and away from the concept of value and worth as a person, which is the essence of satisfaction in sexual relationships, as well as in all other friendships. The return to a perception of value has to come through a healthy loving experience, to which few in this condition are willing to commit themselves. Like the drug addict, the highest priority in their systems concepts – placed above all others – is their addiction which, to the sexual deviant, is physical gratification.

"Commitment is only possible when a person admits the need for help. The sexual deviant and the con artist see the world as having a problem, not themselves. Until a person admits a problem, I know of no way help can be provided. Perhaps you can see why I find working with these people so difficult."

"I understand what you're saying, Ed, but what about the rest of us? What about the people with whom you work? What causes those people to want to evaluate and change their systems concepts?"

"To understand how it happens, you first have to remember that our systems concepts are the basis of all our values and beliefs. All of our decisions and consequent actions derive their directions from these systems and must be in harmony with them. We interact with our environments in an attempt to find satisfaction, and our value systems are our roadmaps or blueprints and have been designed by us to give direction to finding that satisfaction. If we aren't able to find satisfaction over a long period of time, then thinking persons are ultimately led to question their value systems.

"In short, *it's the chronic pain of unresolved conflict that gets us to question our fundamental belief systems.* When our values don't seem to lead us to deal with our environments in such a way that we can derive sufficient satisfaction, the present pain becomes greater than what we're willing to endure. Then we begin to seek help or to search for alternative values to find relief. As one recovering alcoholic friend said recently, 'When you're sick and tired of being sick and tired, you look for an alternative life style.'

"The sexual deviant and the con artist have a whole series of values within their systems concepts which are so completely antagonistic to the social customs and morals of our population that a fundamental change has to be made throughout their entire systems of beliefs. Even with a strong, sincere commitment, this would involve an enormous amount of new experiences upon which to build a whole new systems concept. Remember, the words or symbols we use will always reflect the accumulation of experiences along with our interpretations of them. Even for those determined souls, such as the thirty- or forty-year practicing alcoholics who enter a recovery program, constructing new value systems is a monumental task, especially if they never have had any warm, healthy, non-sexual, long-lasting relational experiences upon which to build new lives."

"Well, you certainly have me questioning my value system. Have you any suggestions for me regarding my problem with self-criticism?"

"I do. I want you to keep a written record of two good things you do every day – things you perceive as having value. It can be simple everyday actions such as combing your hair, taking a bath, saying hello to a friend, smiling at an employee, rubbing your child's back."

"It might sound strange to you, but this isn't going to be that easy," Betty said. "I don't consider those kinds of things to be all that good. You have no idea how critical I am of myself."

"It doesn't have to be the accomplishment of a major life-long goal, Betty," I said smiling, "but I can see you're not going to like the second part of the plan."

"What's that?" she asked.

"Once you've written something down, never list it on any future day. What that means is that you have to think of two different things you do each day that you believe are good, things that have value."

"I could run out of things to list fairly quickly," she said.

"Well, one thing that might help you is that the more specific you are in listing something down, the longer your list can be."

"I don't understand," she said, looking puzzled.

"If you put down 'fixed the evening meal' as something positive, that's very general. I would suggest writing down specific things like 'fixed a salad' or 'sliced up some fruit' or 'baked some potatoes.' These are more specific and will give you more possibilities to write down."

"This sounds like an awfully silly way to deal with what you say is such a serious problem," Betty said skeptically.

"You're right, it does, Betty," I said nodding, "but remember, you have developed patterned ways of looking at yourself, and by your own admission, they're highly critical. The only way to change this pattern is to feed back into your system a constant perception of the good things you do. You'll find that over a period of time, your whole demeanor will begin to change, without your being much aware of it."

"I feel so stupid," Betty said, shrugging her shoulders. "It's just hard to get into my head that you don't want me to deal directly with actions, but rather perceptions and wants. What you're saying sounds logical, I just have a hard time thinking it through and applying it to what you're suggesting. When do you think I will notice a change, and how long do I have to take these notes?"

"To answer the second question first, you should keep making your list until you have developed a strong enough habit of looking at the good things you do. It took one young woman six months before she was comfortable with herself. The average time is about four to six weeks. As I mentioned before, it depends on how committed you are.

"Concerning your first question, you will first notice a great deal of discomfort, and there will be a tendency to deny what you're perceiving. You will sense embarrassment, a sense of hypocrisy that this isn't really you. Ultimately, if you persist, it will work.

"As you continue, others will notice how you have changed, that you seem happier and more relaxed. Your family will notice a reduction in your criticism of them. The woman who took six months until she was comfortable with herself made the million dollar real estate club four years later."

"I'm sure Bob and the children will be happy not to have me on their backs as much," Betty said.

"If you find yourself highly critical of Bob or any of your children, you can change your perception of anyone of whom you're critical by just writing down two things they do every day that are good and do not repeat anything you have written about them. Would you have anyone specifically in mind?"

"Well, I'm very critical of Tim," Betty admitted. "I suppose I should begin with him.

"OK, now you have two lists to make, one for yourself and one for your son, Tim. How about your relationship with Bob, are you willing to work at that?"

"I just don't know, Ed. I was very upset when I walked in here and I realize I haven't been perfect, and you've given me a lot of things to think about – but I really don't think Bob is all that serious, do you?"

"Who initiated coming in for counseling?"

"Yes, I know, it was Bob," she said. "If only this had been 10 years ago, I would have....."

"Betty, do you want to work at improving your marriage?"

"I do and I don't," she said, sounding more confused. "I just don't know anymore."

"Betty, is there someone else?"

Betty breathed deeply for a few moments. "Yes, I guess there is."

"Is it serious?"

"I thought so," she said, speaking in a whisper, tears filling her eyes. "He's manager of another branch. It started out as a friendship. He's having similar problems at home. Lately, over the past few months, we've been having lunch now and then. I can't stop thinking about him, wanting to be with him. I don't know what to do, I've been so confused lately. I can't sleep at night, I've been sick to my stomach, and I'm getting more and more irritable. I just haven't been myself. I don't know what's wrong. I thought seeing Fred would give me a little pleasure in life, but I just am not handling this thing very well anymore. I'm a wreck sometimes."

"Generally when people have a conflict within themselves, they have the symptoms you've been having. What is it that you want?"

Betty looked at me, tears welling up in her eyes. "I would like to be happy, that's all. I'd like to feel good again."

"Is having a relationship with Fred helping you to meet your goal?"

"No, of course it isn't. I feel wonderful when we are together but then later . . ." She trailed off and said nothing. After a few minutes, she continued. "I know it's wrong and hopeless, yet I don't know what to do. I can't stop myself. Every other option I have looks worse."

"Would you be interested in learning how to resolve this problem?"

"Good Lord, yes!" she said, looking directly into my eyes. "I've got to get relief, somehow." Then she took a deep breath, wiped her eyes, and said, "Yes, do go on, you've been really very helpful so far – a lot more than I expected."

"Before we discuss this problem, could I take a moment with you to review what a conflict is and how it works within us?"

"Fine," she answered, "especially if it will help me find some peace within myself. That's really what I'm looking for."

Chapter 6

CONFLICT: THE HEART OF STRESS

"Most conflict is the result of having two incompatible goals," I began. "What this means is that the two things you want, by their very nature, cannot both be achieved. They're mutually exclusive."

"What do you mean?"

"Well, Betty, let's take a look at what you want. You want to stay married, and you want to be with Fred. The conflict comes from your beliefs and values – your systems concept. You probably have within your systems concept the belief that divorce is wrong. If you were to take that route, you would perceive yourself as a failure. What is worse, it would impact how you want to be seen by others, such as your parents, your friends, and people at work. This might reduce your value in the eyes of your supervisors. You probably have a kind of value system that involves keeping the family together to avoid further trauma for your children, especially Ruthie.

"On the other hand, like all of us, I'm sure you have within you a strong urge for value or worth within your home. You've achieved this to some degree at work, but your husband and children, especially Tim, don't show you respect. With the exception of Ruthie, you perceive that they take you for granted. In short, on the one side, there are strong family values, yet there is a deep sense of loneliness and lack of worth as a person. You don't see how you can achieve that feeling of worth within your family.

"As for the other side of the coin, Fred offers you what you aren't getting at home. He's loving toward you, accepts you the way you are, and is no doubt very affectionate. In the privacy of your meetings, he holds you in his arms, making you feel lovable and completed. I'm sure he tells you that you deserve better, listens to your concerns and problems, as I'm sure you listen to his. In a sense, you hold each other's hands, trying to give each other what you both want.

"In addition, since you and Fred hold the same position at the bank, you have a lot in common to discuss, and you both can conveniently arrange your time together without creating any suspicion. He even offers the added benefit of new physical intimacy, which gives the illusion of a possible, highly satisfying, long-term relationship. I'm sure you're both aware of the temporary nature of a new passion for someone, but I'm sure as well that you see the increased affection as a far cry from the cold reception which awaits you at home."

Betty looked at me for awhile, then spoke in a quiet voice. "You certainly know how to read a mind. That's exactly what's happening!"

"Fred's married?" Betty nodded. "Does he want to leave his wife?"

Betty's voice was barely above a whisper. "He said he can't leave because of his children." There was a moment of silence. Then she added, "But he says he can't lose me either."

"Betty." She looked up at me. "The conflict which you feel as stress is being created by the disharmony you're experiencing. You perceive that you can't get everything you want either at home or with Fred. If you look at how we make decisions at program level and the two levels above, systems concept and principle, and see how these three levels are interrelated and dependent on one another, you will realize how critical it is to maintain a certain degree of harmony within the system.

"For example, I'm sure that within your value system there is a strong belief that fidelity and trust, which are part of relational integrity, are critical within marriage. At principle level, therefore, there would be certain standards which would guide your decisions about what to do at program level. When you became intimately involved, what you were doing at program level was in conflict with your standards at principle level and your values, which are at systems concept level."

"It's true that I feel a lot of anxiety and guilt about it," Betty said.

"This is at the heart of all internal conflict. In this case, what you're doing is in direct conflict with a value system or standard you have set for yourself. As I said earlier, any time we want something, two signals are sent out by the brain. One activates the motor muscles so we can achieve what we want. In your case, you have locked yourself into a no-win, can't-decide-what-to-do position. If you move toward Bob and give up Fred, you will have lost the relationship you have that presently brings you a sense of worth. If you move toward Fred, you lose your marriage, which would bring down on you the wrath you expect from your family and friends and put yourself through the resulting hassle."

"I guess that is why I can't sleep, and I'm so irritable," Betty said.

"That has to do with the second signal from the brain. If you remember, I mentioned that the second signal that is activated when we want something goes down to the physiological system in a patterned form, representing all the various levels in the hierarchy. This patterned signal activates the energy management system which produces the energy that's sensed as feelings. We talked about that earlier. This signal continues to produce energy until we have satisfied the system by bringing about an integrated harmony throughout the various levels in the hierarchy.

"The result of this continuous outpouring of energy without its efficient use is that it begins to affect the normal balance of the rest of all our bodily functioning. This excess energy results in numerous symptomatic physiological problems. We find ourselves feeling exhausted yet unable to sleep. We seem easily upset and irritated. A sensation of nervousness develops. Our backs begin to hurt or maybe headaches develop or perhaps our stomachs begin acting up. Our whole world begins to fall apart. We are in conflict and come face to face with the consequent feelings of stress.

"Let me show you how this works. Keep your left hand at your side. Point just your right hand index finger at my two index fingers." I extended both arms, pointed both index fingers at her, and touched them at the tip making a V. "As I move my fingers up and down, all I ask you to do is to keep your index finger pointed directly at both my index fingers. Are you all set?"

"Okay," she replied. I began to move my index fingers in unison up and down. Betty faithfully followed my fingers by moving her right hand up and down, following my movements. Suddenly, I stopped and moved my fingers rapidly apart so that my arms were spread open. Betty stopped, looked puzzled at both my outstretched arms, and began to frown. Her right hand, index finger still extended, stopped moving midway between my fingers. She looked back and forth, first at one finger then the other. Then she looked at me.

"Notice how your actions have stopped. Inside you there is an urge to continue following my instructions, but now you have two incompatible goals. Move closer to either one of my index fingers and you move further away from the other. That is exactly how conflict works in the brain. You want to satisfy two goals, but as you move toward one, you create greater dissatisfaction with the other. What do you do when this happens? You do nothing. You stay in a holding pattern without resolving the conflict, which assures continued misery within your system. The feelings you sense as a result of that conflict are stress. The first source of stress, whether at home, at work, by ourselves or with others is the result of trying to satisfy two incompatible goals.

"The solution to having incompatible goals is to first evaluate your goals and how you prioritize them at the systems concept level. Next decide which is more important. Then you deal with your standards and the decisions you make.

"The second source of stress is when we continually try to satisfy one or more goals over which we have little or no control. This can come through trying, over a long period of time, to accomplish a goal which is physically or mentally unattainable. A person tries out for a football team but he's much too small and hasn't the capacity to stand the tough, physical contact. Trying to accomplish more than we literally have time for is another good example – not being able to take the time to smell the roses. You hear people say, 'My credit card payments are killing me!' Yet who was it that made all the purchases, and who can't figure out how to make the payments?

"A good example is the frustration we experience waiting in heavy traffic. If the car in front of you is moving too slowly, the kids in the back seat are fighting, your spouse is telling you what to do, and you're missing your favorite television program, what is happening inside your head? You want a number of things to happen over which you have little or no control. As your desire for these things increases, the amount of energy being used in your system increases as well. This in turn is overloading your circuits. Your body develops a physical symptom such as a headache and you see those around you as the cause of your discomfort. But in reality, you're the cause. You just want a number of things to be different than they presently are and you have no power to change them at the time.

"One way of dealing successfully with something over which we have no control is by reducing the number of areas that we can reasonably deal with, thus limiting what we want to the bare essentials. When caught in traffic with your children, you could change most of what is going on around you by getting the family to sing songs together or play a game. However, since you perceive them to be the cause of your misery, you may fail to see the possible solutions.

"I read several newspapers a day, but I have stopped watching television news," I told her. "I no longer view all the upset, misery, dishonesty, and unhappiness that goes on. I can do little to change it all, so why watch it and create within myself the added stress? Since I quit TV news, my life is far more serene. I no longer get distraught about the weather, upset that some people had their life savings taken, that a child was beaten, that a home burned down, or that someone was killed in an auto accident. Not only that, I have more time to deal with those things over which I do have control.

"I have a rather sizable electric bill every month, especially in the summer, and so I routinely go around the house, making sure doors are shut, lights are out, and the stove is off. We should show the same vigilance toward our own internal system. We should continually examine the things we want to accomplish, discard those things over which we have no control, and reduce activity in areas which have a low priority in our lives.

"Most people who suffer from excessive feelings of stress tend to look for ways to relax. Many try bio-feedback, self-hypnosis, massage, and other methods of relaxation, which are all very legitimate. Physicians prescribe various medications. The problem is that we need to resolve the internal conflicts which are the causes of stress. What we are doing instead is dealing with the symptoms of the conflict, not the conflict itself. So we lock ourselves into the methods of relaxing we have learned or pills we are taking, and our systems continue on their abusive ways. It just doesn't make much sense to focus on the symptoms of stress and ignore the problem. Obviously, we can't achieve freedom from stress by dealing with the symptoms. We have to get at the root causes."

Betty sighed. "That's me, I'm taking something now for my nerves. And you're right, I never get any time to myself – you know, to do the things I'd like to do. I have stress coming at me from every direction. I guess we haven't talked much about my job. Even though I like my job, it still is very stressful most the time."

"Well, Betty, let's examine your job and see what's going on," I suggested. "From what you've told me thus far, you have a supervisor who has perceived you as being overly critical of others. What else is concerning to you?"

"As a woman manager, I'm at a disadvantage a lot of the time. Employees try to get away with more than with a man, and, when I do insist on their following rules, some take it personally. They act as though my actions are a personal vendetta against them. I have two employees that are never on time and a personal banker whose work output is half of what his peers are doing. I've tried talking to all three of these people many times. A male supervisor would be seen as strict, but his employees probably wouldn't take his criticism personally. I know I'm called a bitch behind my back.

"Then there's the good-old-boy system for both supervisors and customers. It's unheard of for a woman, married or single, to call several male customers and invite them to play golf. The same thing goes on between my peers and supervisors. If I were a man, it would be acceptable for me to do so. That network helps a branch manager deal with the departments which provide services to that branch. I've been having problems with the charge card division downtown at the main office. These people are constantly making mistakes which take us forever to correct. Several of the male branch managers play golf with the supervisor of that division. You can guess who is going to get greater cooperation in solving this problem.

"I must admit that things are getting better since they started a new networking system within our bank recently. All the managers have been involved in various classes and meetings, often conducted by women. This has allowed for increased networking between men and women, not only at our bank but throughout the banking industry. Nowadays, it seems to be evolving into the entire business community.

"I suppose that I make problems for myself. Sometimes when my secretary is away from her desk, I look through the files for something I want. If she's away for the day, I might even type some letters that need to go out immediately. I guess by taking on the technical work others should be doing I create the impression of having less authority than the male branch managers. I'm sure a man would get someone else to hunt down what he's looking for or would have someone else type his letters." Betty stopped abruptly. She seemed upset.

"I'll teach you how to deal with your employees later, but first we need to discuss what it is that you *want*. I'm going to ask you to list those things you want in relation to the problems you have been mentioning, both at home and at work." I jotted Betty's list on the chalk board.

What Betty wants:
Bob to show me more love
Tim to stop using foul language
Mike to stop drinking
June to get rid of Charlie
Employees to show more respect
Employees to come in on time

"Betty, how many of the things that you have listed here do you have control over getting?"

"What do you mean?"

"Let me ask this first, what is the one desire you think we all have in common – that all of us want?"

"Well, I suppose everyone wants to be happy," she said slowly.

"In other words, everyone wants to feel good, enjoy the kind of life they perceive as satisfying," I said, confirming her remark. "So, everything you want is really an attempt to feel good?"

"Well, of course," she said.

"Does it make more sense to try to change things over which you have control or those things over which you have no control?"

"Naturally, those things over which I have control," she said.

"I agree. Why give someone else control over how you feel by making what you want dependent on what others do or think? It doesn't make sense, does it?"

"Of course not!"

"Let's take a look at your list and see whether you have control over the things you have said you want so that you could be happy."

Betty looked at the list. She said nothing for a few moments, then said in a surprised voice, "I see what you're saying. I really don't have much control in those areas where I'm trying to find happiness, do I?"

"Do you have any control at all?"

"None, I guess," she said, looking dismayed. "I guess I've been trying to find happiness through wanting things I don't have control over. It sounds so foolish, doesn't it?"

"Betty, every time we make a decision to achieve a goal, we are operating at the program level. This is the level where you decide what you want to get in specific terms. However, this level only reflects the higher levels above it."

"I think I'm with you," she said, although still looking puzzled.

"Remember, the systems concept level, which is the highest level, is where we decide what is important to us such as our values. It's from these values that we set our standards which, in turn, we use as a guide when we decide what actions to take. For example, you want a loving relationship in your marriage, you want children happily seeking their own destiny, and you want to be a successful and productive manager at work. From what we have talked about so far, these are the general areas in which you look to enhance your life and find satisfaction."

"Well, yes, that's the way I would like things to be," she agreed.

"Since you haven't listed any areas over which you have control, what I want you to do now is to list the general areas of satisfaction that are reflected in what you want. In other words, what areas within your systems concept would these wants be trying to satisfy?"

Betty frowned. "I'm confused. Would you give me an example?"

"Take the first want on your list. 'Bob to show more love.' This suggests you would like to be happier in your relationship with Bob, would it not? So, your area of satisfaction would be love or belonging."

"Oh, I see what you mean. My wants are those particular things within my systems concept that would collectively come under the heading of love or belonging. By trying to get Bob to love me more I'm trying to find satisfaction in those areas, Bob being the specific person."

"I couldn't have said it better. Within our systems concepts or value systems you can cluster the concepts into certain areas of satisfaction. Perhaps individual relationships at work, home, and elsewhere might be grouped under *love*. Families, groups, and even the people at your branch bank could be called *belonging*. So when you state a specific want, it really reflects a more general want within your systems concept, which in turn can be classified as belonging to one of the various areas of your life. Some people call them *needs*. We'll talk more about those later.

"So let's see if you can determine for yourself an area of satisfaction within your systems concept that reflects your other wants." Betty worked at her list for a few minutes.

What Betty wants:	**any control?**	**area of satisfaction**
Bob to show me more love	no	love & belonging
Tim to stop using foul language	no	love & belonging
Mike to stop drinking	no	love & belonging
June to get rid of Charlie	no	happiness for child
Employees to show more respect	no	value & worth
Employees to get along with each other	no	value & worth

"Now, Betty, since you want to develop a sense of control over how you feel, then controlling how you feel comes from being able to accomplish what you want. Is there an alternative pathway that you could choose to find satisfaction in the area of love and belonging?" Betty thought for a minute. "When Bob and I were dating, we used to take long walks together," she said wistfully. "We were always doing things together. I keep thinking of how I criticized him for suggesting a walk last evening. I really got mad at him. I now see what he wanted." She was silent for a minute, then added, "Well, I could ask him to take a walk this evening, that's something we haven't done in a long, long time."

"What if he refuses?"

"Well, at least I'll have tried," she said, sighing. "I wish I had gone last night." She sat up a little straighter. "I know, I'll go for the walk myself. No, I'll ask Ruthie to take a walk. She's always wants someone to do something with her."

"Now you're thinking," I said, grinning. "You're choosing alternatives over which you have some control. In Bob's case, you're asking him to take a walk. If he says no, which he might very well do, then you have an alternative plan to walk with Ruthie. Do you see how you're taking control over how you feel? Since you have control over getting what you want through an alternative pathway, you're in complete control over how you feel."

"Yes, I can see that," she answered. "But how do I deal with my feelings of guilt over Mike's drinking? I feel responsible. Bob and I both stopped going to church years ago, when Mike was a small child, so I feel responsible for the lack in his moral upbringing. Also, Bob drinks a lot of beer, and I used to have a glass of wine before and during dinner. I guess we haven't been good examples no matter which way you turn. I feel so guilty every time I see him take a drink."

"Betty, can I get you to do what you don't want to do?"

"Well, no, no one can," she said.

"Can you cause your children to take on a certain personality, to be a certain way?"

"Well, no, I guess not," she said.

"Does June drink?"

"No, she doesn't want anything to do with it," she responded. "June refuses to come around when Mike is home."

"Did you ever consciously try to make Mike drink, encourage him in any way?"

"No, of course not," she said.

"Do the ideas I've been teaching you – that we build our own world and create our own desires – make sense to you?"

"Yes, they really do," she said. "It's still a little confusing, but I can see how each person determines what she wants and how she feels. I can really see that."

She paused for a moment, as if she were thinking to herself, then added, "From what you said about alcoholism a few minutes ago, Mike could very well be addicted. Isn't there anything I can do?"

"Could you have forced Bob to seek counseling?" I asked.

"No, certainly not," she said, then added, "I guess Mike will have to find his own way back, is that it?"

"Mike cannot be helped by you or anyone unless he sincerely wants help. That's the bottom line. If you want more help in understanding how to deal with Mike, then you should find an Alanon group. These groups teach through sharing experiences with family members and friends how to understand and deal with the alcoholic. However, this group does more than that. Often those who live and deal with alcoholics need help themselves, for most of them behave in such a way as to enable alcoholics to continue in their addiction. At the end of our session, I'll give you a name of an Alanon group to call if you wish help in dealing with Mike."

"I guess for anyone, it really comes down to a matter of control," Betty said thoughtfully. "What you're saying is that for me to be happy, I have to learn to take responsibility for those things over which I have control, otherwise how I feel is being determined by someone else."

"You've sized it up really well," I said.

"Yet there seems to be something missing in all this," Betty said. "I don't know how to explain it, but how do we figure out what to do when we don't know what to do? Some people seem to work their own ways out of difficulties, like the creative process you always hear so much about."

"Betty, you're very perceptive. What you're asking about is something I rarely discuss because it's so complicated. Yet it's fascinating. Let me see if I can help you understand the reorganization system."

Chapter 7

REORGANIZATION:
THE MIND'S REPAIR KIT

"Betty, when you started at the bank, did you know anything about banking?" I asked.

"Well, now that I'm a branch manager, I can honestly say no," Betty said, laughing. "I thought I did, but I really didn't know anything."

"That's pretty much how we are when we are born. Only, as infants, it's the environment around us that we struggle to understand. Within what is called our behavioral hierarchies, which consist of the levels we have been talking about, there are three areas. First, we have the levels of our perceptual systems that create an understanding of our environments and ourselves. Second, we have memory that stores the information as we construct it. Third, there are all the various levels of wants that determine our actions. It's our actions, in turn, that help us deal with our environment and bring us satisfaction in our lives by getting us what we want. At birth, and probably to some degree while we are in our mother's womb, we begin to create these individual and unique worlds.

"My guess is that this is how you entered the world of banking. You probably developed your own ideas of what banking was all about, depending on your experiences with the departments in which you worked and the people for whom you worked. Most of what we learn is similar to what others learn, although this new information will be altered by our own unique ways of perceiving things. Children growing up in a family learn about the same foods, but everybody has favorites as well as those things they just can't stand.

"At the same time, I'm sure that your bank has a system that senses any lack of harmony between your branch and the goals of the various departments that oversee all the branches."

"You'd better believe it," Betty said. "We have the sales department letting us know when our sales goals aren't being met, division managers sensing when the budgets aren't in order, and a customer service department that jumps down our throats when we have too many complaints. No matter who I hear from, it's the same demand – 'It's out of order, fix it.' " Then she smiled and added, "You sound as if you have some knowledge of the banking system yourself."

"I have several friends at the bank I use," I admitted. "But, getting back to my analogy, our bodies have somewhat similar designs. The internal operations of your branch are similar to that part of us that figures out what has to be done to operate efficiently. I am speaking here of the hierarchy of levels in perceptions and wants that we have been discussing. We also have a sensing system that is designed to recognize when there is disharmony within our system, and it acts on our system in an attempt to help it re-establish harmony within itself. This is called the **reorganization system** which has a function similar to the various outside departments you just mentioned. Here's a diagram of the reorganization system." I handed her a piece of paper.

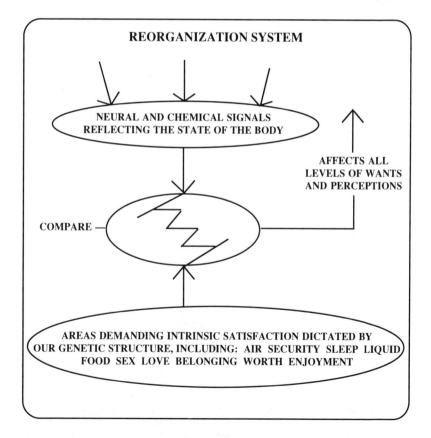

"We've talked about the chronic and increasingly painful conflict that comes from having either two incompatible goals or trying to satisfy goals over which we have little or no control. When that happens, there is a chronic excess of energy generated in the physiological organs as a result of the unresolved conflicts. This excessive energy is sensed by the perceptual system as an overwhelming overload of emotional sensation. This feeling is what is called *stress*."

"How well I know that feeling," Betty said. "both at work and at home. Even when I try to escape from my family and my work, I still have to deal with the stress. Last week I had taken a day's vacation time. I was going to sleep in, be alone in the house, and pamper myself. So what happened? Bob called from work and informed me he had taken my car because his wouldn't start. After that, my daughter called crying about something her boyfriend did. Then Tim called from school wanting me to come pick him up because he'd been suspended for smoking. Finally, my assistant manager called saying the audit department wanted me to call 'right away.' That's stress."

"How did you cope with it?"

"I said the heck with them all, and I ignored everyone. I went into my bedroom, got undressed, and took a nice, hot bath," she said. "It was too much. I was stressed out before all this happened. That's why I had taken the day off. I had needed to get away from all of them, and I wasn't willing to deal with all the demands on my free time."

"Good for you," I said, laughing. "As you saw in that situation, the greater the number of conflicts we have to deal with at once, the more dramatically the pressure increases within our systems to reduce the pain of unresolved conflicts."

"I felt like I was going to go crazy," Betty said. "I was so overwhelmed, I couldn't think of what to do. I just took a bath. I might add that it felt great! But how are you supposed to deal with all this conflict? My bath was relaxing, but it didn't solve anything."

"You first have to set your priorities within your systems concept level and then set some standards for what you want to resolve. But before I review all that with you, let me describe what the reorganization system does and doesn't do. Ordinarily, when we have a problem and we have a method for solving it, we would use the method and eliminate the problem. I am sure many of your audit problems involve a logical procedure for dealing with an out-of-balance account."

"That's right," Betty said, nodding.

"When you have a problem, and you don't know what to do, and you have no prior experience to rely on, then you have to reorganize. However, this system within us is not an intelligent system, and it doesn't figure out your problems for you. Frankly, it can't. It's not designed that way. Rather, what it does is alter, in a very fundamental way, how you perceive things. A whole host of ideas flow through your mind in a totally indiscriminate way, revealing new directions to take.

"Scientists are still researching how all this happens. There is evidence, however, that the strength of the electro-chemical neural signals within the brain are altered at the points where they connect. These connections are called synapses. These changes produce a variety of perceptual signals in a totally random and unorganized pattern. As these various thoughts race through our mind, some will be sensible, some not, some weird, some stupid, some frightening, some helpful. We can then freely select from these many available options.

"Regardless of how this works, the effect of reorganization is like thinking about something and a new way of perceiving a former thought may flash into your mind. All of a sudden you see things with a different understanding. Something just pops into your head. You get a new idea to consider, an alternative that just might work. You feel more like your former self. You begin to relax again. We've all had that experience."

Betty looked straight at me as though I had just read her mind. She seemed to understand what I was saying. "When I started seeing Fred – not at the branch meetings, but alone and in more secluded places – I began to feel a great deal of discomfort. After I began going to bed with him, this feeling of stress became much more pronounced. I can't tell you the extreme pressure I felt, that I put myself under. Frankly, it's been a living hell!

"On the one hand, there is my family, my position at the bank, and my marriage, such as it is." She paused reflectively. "It's hard to throw away the tradition of a lifetime. It's where all my values reside – at least I believe they do. Then, on the other hand, there is my time with Fred. He's so very kind and loving, so understanding. He makes me feel more like a woman, more appreciated. That's awfully hard to walk away from. When you were describing conflict a few minutes ago, this was all I could think of. I've tried to think of a way out, but I just stay confused. I don't like what I'm doing with Fred, but I can't stand my home life. It has gotten to the point where I don't want to look at myself in the mirror any more."

I paused a few seconds, pushing the box of tissues closer to Betty. "To some counselors, this would be a time to dig for more feelings. To me, it's a time to teach. O.K.?"

Betty nodded, and I continued, "The discomfort you're talking about is caused by the desire of your internal system to maintain internal harmony. As that dissatisfaction continues or increases, ultimately you will begin to reorganize. This system doesn't react quickly, but only after the pain becomes chronic or increasingly unbearable. When you need a certain amount of food, water, or sleep, your body sets up a disturbance in your system which you long ago learned to recognize as hunger, thirst, or tiredness. In the same way, your system demands internal harmony in all areas that you have identified as being important to you.

"What was making you explore and sift through the various ideas you have had to resolve your problem was this intrinsic system of yours that continually attempts to maintain harmony. Because you are in a state of conflict, things are changing fast. During this time, I'm sure you've felt very distressed and upset because, when you're reorganizing, your whole system is going to reflect that lack of harmony. We hate these feelings of stress, this sense of not knowing, of incoherence, of disorganization, which is caused by our unresolved conflicts. The reorganization system responds to this sense of not being in harmony. One of the consequences of all this is that you sometimes have feelings that don't make any sense. In fact, lots of things may not make sense for a while because this particular experience is so new.

"Right now, you are struggling to learn new ideas about yourself and better ways of functioning with Bob, your children, and your work. Though it may be exciting, it's also kind of unpleasant because these new ideas tend to make a mess out of how you have understood things to be. It's being faced with incongruence in your intellectual world and having to set new goals and standards that's so unsettling. This need for harmony or internal consistency makes you aware of when you have this internal peace, and you surely know when you don't."

"If this system doesn't know how to figure out our problems, then how does it know what answers to suggest to our mind?" Betty asked.

"It doesn't. It's a dumb system," I said, laughing a little. "Our reorganization system senses that something must be done, so it randomly alters the electrical strength of our neural signals, which contain and transmit our perceptions. This forms and triggers new combinations of neural circuits. By breaking connections and making new ones, our reorganization system produces an unlimited and uncontrolled variety of different perceptions at all of the various levels in our behavioral hierarchy. You select and reject these various ideas according to how you perceive things and what you want."

"Do you mean the ideas that come to us are totally random?" Betty asked, with a note of surprise.

"Right, and sometimes really crazy thoughts occur! Let me ask you, as you've been trying to deal with the inconsistency within your marriage, what has been going on in your mind?"

"You're right about crazy thoughts," she said. "I've had a lot of ideas come to mind that are really stupid when I think about them. I thought about just leaving home, letting Bob handle the problems at home, turning the kids over to him. I've thought about just staying in my room and not coming out anymore. I've thought of leaving town, going somewhere to start all over, getting Fred to leave town with me. Then I've had some really crazy thoughts involving violence. As you said, it's the uncertainty of it all. You certainly have put your finger on my problem."

"That's part of what I do, help people understand how their systems function. My main job is to teach you how to use your system in such a way that you can return to a tranquil state and maintain that harmony.

"The reorganization system not only helps us when we are in conflict, but it is also used in the creative thinking process. When I'm writing, I often dwell on an idea I'm struggling with for several days, sometimes weeks, until I understand it clearly. It took me four or five years to understand control theory sufficiently so I could write about it. As a counselor, I see myself primarily as an aid to teaching my clients how their system works and then helping them to develop confidence in the use of their own reorganization systems, which include their creative processes."

"Right now, I am just interested in getting things resolved," Betty said. Then she seemed to relax a little and added, "However, I can see how I have used this at work. Occasionally when I have to write a report, I have difficulty thinking through what I want to say. So I get up from my desk and wander around the branch. Then sometimes something comes to me, and I can get my report written. Am I using that system then?"

"Yes, you are."

"Well, then, from now on, when I have a problem, I'll just turn the reorganization system on and wait for the solution," Betty said.

"I'm afraid it can't be turned on at will. There are many creative writers, composers, and all sorts of artists who will testify to that. As a writer, I can tell you that it isn't something you can turn on and off like a faucet. You have to wait until the system makes up it's mind to do so. You can't force it.

"However, what you can do is review what you know. You can look over what you have written, and you can keep talking things through in your mind. Then, all of a sudden, you say 'wait a minute.' And it's there. When I'm home alone is my best time, because there are no distractions. I look out the window, go out and water a few plants, look at the mountains in the distance. Sometimes I don't do anything. I've finally learned the sometimes frustrating lesson of having to sit around and wait for it to happen.

"When I wanted to write a book on stress, I somehow sensed my mind wasn't ready. Several months later, when I told Hester I wanted to do it, I still wasn't ready. Then, all of a sudden, months later, I felt that I was ready. But, whether I am waiting to write a book or just for an idea to come along, when it does happen, all of a sudden, I feel something sort of gather itself together within me, and I go turn on my computer, sit down, start writing, and there it is. Frankly, I don't feel as if I have had very much of a hand in the whole operation. My responsibility is to sift through the ideas once they appear in my mind and decide how they should be expressed.

"As you've testified, Betty, this is also true when there is serious internal conflict. I had one divorced single parent tell me she was in conflict for a full year after her husband left. Finally, one day, she just saw herself as over the divorce – able to cope with her daily problems."

"I hope that it's not that long for me," she said sadly.

"The beginning of the end is when you make a firm commitment in a certain direction. When the conflict is sensed, the system turns on and stays on until the sensed signals from the conflict begin to subside and harmony is restored once again to the system. Once you decide what your values are, set your priorities within that system, set standards to reflect your beliefs, and evaluate your actions against the newly established criteria, you will begin to sense the relief you're seeking. Over time, if you don't experience any improvement, then you have to re-evaluate your system.

"When it comes to creativity, that's different. Sometimes you sit and wait for your mind to come up with something, and nothing appears. Then, all of a sudden, in the middle of taking a shower or when you're talking with a friend or washing the dishes or looking out the window, something comes to you. This reorganization system is very independent and has a 'mind of its own.' Remember, it is a genetically built-in, internal sensing system and is not directly controlled by our wants and perceptions. It works according to its own rules."

"What is the difference between the reorganization system and the strong desires we get, such as needs?" Betty asked. "It seems to me that's part of what you are talking about, isn't it?"

"If you define a need as something within us that tells us what to do when something is wrong, I don't believe such a thing exists. But, if you are looking at needs as those desires that *let us know when something is wrong* within our system, then the reorganization system is strongly related to needs. In other words, needs may recognize the problem, but we have to figure out how to resolve it.

"We have learned to identify specific feelings having to do with our physical needs, such as the need for food, sleep, and water. We learn early in life the precise meaning of the feelings of hunger, thirst, and exhaustion by comparing our own prior experiences with these inner feelings. Thus, our physical needs are defined by our own intrinsic systems and are satisfied by our own actions, independent of others. Even in infancy, when someone else provides food, water, or a place to sleep, we activate our own behaviors of eating, drinking, or sleeping which satisfy our internal intrinsic systems.

"The feelings we experience when we do not fill the need for satisfaction for what we call love or worth is quite another problem. These feelings we satisfy mostly by our interactions with others. I can't satisfy my desire for a human relationship unless I find someone else who is willing to do the same with me, but I can eat an apple, drink some water, or take a nap, and I really don't need anyone to help me."

Betty looked thoughtful. "That's true, but you certainly recognize the problem when you feel lonely, don't you?"

"In a way, that's true, Betty. You recognize that something is wrong. The problem is that many counselors fail to understand the fact that each person constructs a personal and specific meaning for a word from that person's own unique experiences. We identify these experiences at category level."

Betty looked puzzled. "What do you mean?"

"Is your meaning of *love,* or any other of these so-called needs, defined by your intrinsic system the same as it is defined by mine? Or, is your idea of *love* defined by you according to the way you constructed your understanding of close relationships, both within as well as outside your family? That is the critical question."

Her expression went blank. "You want to go over that again?"

"I know when I feel lonely, because I know how I have defined loneliness. The question is this: what makes the same relationship acceptable to one spouse and unacceptable to the other?" I asked.

"I don't know," Betty said. "I guess I look at marriage a lot differently than he does."

"You're absolutely right," I said. "As we build our perceptual world and determine for ourselves what is important to us, we define concepts within our systems about the kind of committed love relationship, usually marriage, that we want. We set standards that reflect our specific kind of marriage and the kind of actions compatible with those standards. We define our ideas of love within the marriage state.

"Betty, supposing Hester has experienced a close, loving relationship within her family, and I never have. The two of us are going to have very different ideas of love because of our past experiences, which is the basis of any symbol we create. Since neither of us can see the other's perception of love, then the kind of experiences we want to have with each other are going to be different. We won't understand that difference because *we can't perceive another's experiences.* We're each going to wonder what's wrong with the other."

"Then why does courtship work?" Betty asked, looking puzzled.

"When we are courting someone, we tend to work at being nice and accommodating, allowing for differences. The experience of someone new, especially the sexual awareness, provides an illusion of security in the relationship.

"The biggest problem during courtship is that we talk the only way we can, in symbols, and *we interpret the words that another uses according to our own experience.* Because our experiences are the only meaning we have had for the words being used, it is hard for us to realize that our intended partner's words reflect totally different experiences from ours. The most effective way I know to integrate our ideas of love with our spouse's is through continual, common experiences over the years, which I have defined as quality time. During our marriages, as our values change and our lives develop, we change. Our love will continue to stay strong only if we continue this process of integrating our experiences. Most people never find out this difference in how love is perceived until after the marriage vows are spoken."

Her eyes lit up. "And that get's back to the value of building standards for the kind of person you want prior to getting married."

"That's right, Betty. Experience is the foundation on which all our words are based. To talk in symbols, or words, which are at category level, without any knowledge of the experience upon which the words are based, is nothing more than creating illusions or a short trip to fantasy land. When you marry someone with the same cultural background, from the same neighborhood, or from the same small community where everyone knows everyone else, it assures at least some similar experiences. There are more likely to be fewer illusions.

"We also build over time our ideas of other kinds of one-on-one relationships, such as those with close friends, parents, brothers and sisters, children, and our colleagues at work. All these defined relationships are clustered into the area we call love, with varying ideas of what they should be like and the standards that reflect those ideas. This is how we build our ideas of love, through our experiences with others."

"So far, I'm with you," Betty said, nodding.

"The way you and Bob have been interacting recently is not consistent with your value system, your idea of the way you think a married relationship should be. Since married love comes under your general heading of love, this lack of satisfaction or disharmony in a relationship will become evident within the physiological system through the kind of energy manufactured according to the patterned signals coming from the behavioral hierarchy."

"Explain some more," Betty said.

"Do you remember how feelings occur? Any time we want something, two signals are sent out from our brain. One activates the motor muscles so we can interact with our environment to satisfy what we want. The other patterned signal activates the energy management system within our organs to produce the various substances that provide the energy so we can accomplish what we want. If you and Bob were doing well, you would sense this energy as the feeling of love. In your present situation, you are not doing well. Thus, you sense this energy as the feeling of loneliness or the absence of love. The patterned effects of this message as it interacts within the physiological organs not only produces this energy, but this is a way the reorganization system recognizes that something is wrong. There is also evidence it recognizes the signals that reflect the differences between what we want and our perceptions. However, the reorganization system is slow to 'kick in'. Our own conflict has to become increasingly painful and chronic.

"The system continues to reorganize and create random perceptual signals until harmony is restored. If we ignore our problems, the discomfort will continue. But, if we focus on the area of our concerns and maintain open attitudes towards the various perceptual thoughts and images that appear to our conscious minds, ultimately an idea will come to us that will, in our judgement, make sense to try. Sooner or later, we will discover something that, when tried, will bring relief and our systems will once again be restored to harmony.

"Remember, the patterned signal being sent reflects the area of concern. If it has to do with how you deal with an employee, the variety of ideas flowing through your consciousness is going to reflect that specific area of difficulty. You aren't going to be thinking of your alcoholic son or your cold and uncaring husband.

"I think I understand what you are saying," Betty said, leaning forward with interest. "What happens when you have many things on your mind at one time?"

"That's the benefit of first reflecting on what is important to you, as found in your systems concept, and setting your priorities at that level. When you begin with the highest prioritized item first, assuming that is where you are having the most frustrating problems, you become aware of the ideas that the reorganization system generates in that area."

"So, when I arrived, Ed, I was looking at every problem and limiting my ability to take some action by trying to deal with all my difficulties at one time. That's why you tried to find out what is most important to me and what I wanted to deal with first."

"You're right about the need to focus on a particular problem, Betty. However, sometimes the most important problem is often the hardest with which to deal. I always try to deal with the highest priority problem, providing that it is easily solved and the client wants to deal with it. You came in here with a very low self-esteem in the area of relationships. I don't want to do anything that is going to jeopardize your chances for improvement. It is a judgement call on my part, assuming you're willing to go along. I don't want you to fail if I can possibly prevent it. I want you to succeed. Nothing breeds higher self-esteem like success.

"In your case, I find you to be a highly successful woman in your career. Fortunately, because Bob wants to work at your marriage and you want to work at building your own self-esteem, I can easily direct you into the areas of both your marriage and yourself. Sometimes I move people into areas over which they have the most control or where they are most likely to succeed and set aside those areas where they are less likely to succeed until they have built sufficient confidence through succeeding in other areas of their lives.

"Getting back to how we define our needs, do you understand what I have said so far?" I asked.

"Well, yes, I guess so," Betty said, cautiously.

"All that I am saying, Betty, is that our systems concepts reflect the way we think things ought to be, and this includes any and all areas of our lives that we have thought about. If you wanted to categorize or cluster these areas into specific segments and call them *needs,* then you might find it easier to understand the meaning of what many call *needs.*

"I have already mentioned a number of areas that would include the concept *love. Belonging* might have to do with all those areas where we feel a part of a group, be it our family, the branch where you manage, or any group where you all have something in common and with whom you interact."

"I see. For example, a bowling league – or friends with whom you exercise?" she suggested.

"Right. Then there's the cluster of beliefs that might have to do with our faith, our relationship with God, and how we should acknowledge that faith through our actions. There's a large cluster having to do with how we gain worth through our various activities and from our importance to others.

"The real danger comes when we try to set limits on what *love* is, what *belonging* is, and perceive them as measurements which everyone else should use. When dealing with actual needs, such as hunger, thirst, and sleep, once we have learned to sense correctly the body's demand for satisfaction in these areas, relief is easily accomplished. Interestingly, in these areas we accept the fact that some people need more sleep than others or that some are satisfied with less food than others.

"When you begin to describe such areas as love, belonging, and worth as needs, the body's demand for satisfaction in these areas is going to depend on the standards that each of us has described for ourselves. When it comes to our need for water or sleep, our body has its own built-in monitoring system. I think we define our own standards for how much love is satisfying and the things we do that give us a sense of worth.

"Obviously we have a lot in common with others, but still there is that unique difference between people that makes their particular systems concepts their own. Systems concept is the level at which we construct the various areas of satisfaction, which include our ideas of love, belonging or worth. Principles level is where we set the guidelines or standards that reflect those needs and upon which we determine the actions that will lead to the satisfaction of those ideas."

Betty raised one finger and said, "So when Bob and I got married, we each had our own individual ideas of the way marriage should be and the standards that reflected those ideas. We didn't have the foresight to compare our individual standards with each other – or to measure our own standards for the kind of spouse we wanted against a prospective spouse. Then we were surprised and unhappy to learn that we had married someone quite different from our standards. In fact, it came as a real shock to me that he didn't turn out to be what I wanted at all."

"It happens to most of us, Betty. But don't worry, it's possible to turn this all around and build a better marriage. Many people I have worked with have shown the willingness to rebuild their marriages, and many have succeeded. It takes a very strong commitment and the kind of persistence that you both seem to exhibit in your jobs."

"If we each have different values and standards, how is it possible for us to reconcile those differences?" Betty asked.

"As you begin to spend quality time with Bob, your perception of him will change. If you recall, the symbols for how you perceive Bob are constructed at category level, based on your experiences as they are perceived at the first six levels. There is nowhere else you can build a valid symbol except through an experience. Changing or improving your category level idea of Bob *has to begin with experiencing Bob.* I don't know how else you can do it. As you and Bob experience each other, the category *Bob* in your head is bound to change. Quality time is the major component in redefining that experience.

"Normally, your commitment to the marriage will strengthen as your perception of him as a warm and attractive person increases. Then, all of a sudden, you will begin to sense a closeness which, hopefully, you will continue to work at maintaining, a closeness called an intimate friendship. Many couples struggle to reach that goal, but it can happen more easily through quality time. Frankly, I know of no other way a warm, loving relationship can be built.

"There are exceptions to this strengthening process which generally reflect a weak commitment. If you wanted to end up with Fred more than you wanted to give your marriage to Bob a chance to improve, this would become evident as you practiced quality time. Spending enjoyable time with Bob alone every day is bound to increase your sense of closeness with him. If Fred is really the one you want, you will work against this increased feeling of intimacy with Bob, and you will no longer want to work at quality time, or you will see it as just performing an unpleasant task. Eventually Bob will sense your lack of commitment.

"However, when there is a commitment, quality time not only helps us construct a more enriching perception of a close relationship, it also serves to protect the integrity of the couple's love. The more satisfied we are in our marriage, the less inclination we have for looking around for another partner.

"Another benefit of this increased intimacy is that we are more inclined to view our marriages as the number one priority in our systems concepts. We are then less likely to allow our jobs, our children, or other important values to interfere with our relational time together. When marriages are given a low priority and problems in other areas arise, people tend to quit working at getting along with their spouses and concentrate their efforts on the troubled area. A close relationship can offer tremendous support when couples struggle with the difficulties elsewhere in their lives. There is just nothing that takes the place of the quality-time experience to establish or rebuild an intimate friendship between two human beings."

"All this time I thought it was just our not being able to communicate that was our problem," Betty said, shaking her head.

"Talking about what you think, your feelings, how upset you are about prior experiences – all this communication is at category level and above. All you are doing is exposing your ideas to another, but they have no basis, no foundation for meaning to the other person. The process for developing and maintaining a closeness with another can only come through integrated action. There is absolutely no way a relationship is going to be rebuilt without having experienced your partner. This is a very fundamental part of the integrating process of two human beings. There's no substitute for quality time alone together."

"When I walked in here, I felt like I was being sucked into a black hole with little hope of escape. Now it seems, from what you have been teaching me, that there is a possibility." She sighed a little and then continued, "I don't know, Bob seems to get depressed so easily, and I get angry all the time. I don't know. I just need to get rid of this anger, and then maybe I could decide."

"What is it that is causing the anger?" I asked.

"You said it earlier. It's the conflict within me," she said. "It's so hard to concentrate on dealing with what I can control when the pain of anger continues to call attention to itself. All I can think about is how angry I am."

"Unfortunately, most people in conflict tend to get involved in their symptoms and deal with them as though they were the cause of their problems. I recently had a young woman here who was bulimic. Rather than talk with her about her symptomatic problem – her eating disorder – I helped her deal with and resolve several conflicts with which she was struggling. She hated her job, her marriage was about to end, and she had a very low self-image.

"As with you, I taught her how to deal with her self-image, which began to improve within the first month. At the same time, she and her husband began to strengthen their marriage through quality time. Since her husband had a well-paying professional job, she left her job and went back to school to earn a degree in social work. With all the improvements, the symptomatic problem, bulimia, disappeared."

"I never really thought of what we do as symptomatic of a conflict," Betty said. "I know that when I get upset or feel a little depressed I generally head for the kitchen."

"I had a client tell me recently that, as her self-image began to improve through writing two good things she did every day, she began to lose weight without even thinking about her diet. As she began to resolve her conflict, her symptomatic behavior – overeating – began to subside. Our internal conflicts have to be resolved if we are ever to find relief from our symptoms. The worst thing that can happen to anyone is to grow old and remain conflicted. The key to growing old gracefully is to be constantly alert to conflicts as they arise and to take care of them before they overwhelm us."

I paused. "Well, Betty, since you are not satisfied with your life the way it is, would you like to work at making it better?"

"Yes, and I would like to try that self-image program that you suggested," she said.

"Would you like to work at your marriage, which means, not seeing Fred?" I asked.

Betty paused. "Yes, I guess so."

"Are you sure?"

"I guess that didn't sound like a very strong commitment, did it?" she said, looking up. "No, I'm sure. If it works out, I'll have a lot more to gain."

"Since Bob understands the concept of quality time, I would suggest you begin this evening, perhaps with a walk. Remember the rules during quality time."

"Yes, I know. No criticism and no going into the negative past," she said, smiling. "I think I'll also commit myself to spending some quality time with Ruthie. She's always trying to get us to play games with her. It seems as though she's already figured out the secret to relationships."

"I'd like to see you and Bob next Monday at five p.m. Is that convenient for you?"

"Yes, and thanks for your help," Betty said, reaching out to shake hands.

"Betty, call me tomorrow and let me know what you and Bob do tonight and also what you put on your list. Here's the phone number to call if you're still interested in learning more about an Alanon group. Also, here's a copy of my quality time card. Bob has one."

"You really do intend for us to make it, don't you?"

I nodded.

Chapter 8

A TIME TO RECHARGE

On the following Monday I saw Bob and Betty together for the first time. As they entered my office and sat down, I asked, "How have things been going?"

"Well, I think things are better," Bob began with some hesitation. He looked at Betty.

"Betty, how about you? Do you think things have improved?"

"Well, yes, I think they have," she answered in a more positive tone.

"How have they improved?" I asked, continuing to look at Betty.

"Well, I don't know. I'm not sure," she said, looking puzzled. "Bob and I have started taking walks in the morning before we leave for work. That seems to be helping."

"How has that helped?" I asked.

Betty continued to look puzzled. Bob replied, "There seems to be a little less tension, you know, we feel more relaxed with each other."

"Yes, that's it," Betty said, nodding. "It seemed pretty strange the first morning. It was like taking a walk with a stranger, but, after twenty minutes or so, it was more relaxed."

"Have you noticed anything else?" I asked.

"When we get home after work, there's still a lot of stress," Bob said. "I must admit, though, we haven't fought as much this week."

"That's true about the stress," Betty added. "And Bob is right about the arguing. We've only had one serious fight."

"When was that?"

"Thursday evening, when Bob said he was too tired to play cards when Ruthie asked him. I was fixing dinner, or I would have played with her – but Bob wouldn't help with that either!" There was a trace of anger in Betty's voice.

"How quickly did you get over the anger you felt when Bob didn't do what you wanted?"

"Ordinarily it would have lasted several days," Betty said without anger this time. "But about half way through our walk Friday morning, I began to feel better. By the time the walk was over, I was over being upset at Bob. That night, he even helped me with the dishes."

"So your anger seems to subside a lot more quickly. Is that it?"

"Well, I never thought of it till now, but, yes, I guess you're right," she answered.

"Could I see the list of what you both have been doing together?"

"Here's the list," Betty said, handing me two pieces of paper. "And here's the list that you told me to keep concerning two things I do every day that are good. Last night, I told Bob about it."

"We missed our quality time on two days – Thursday and Saturday – but otherwise we did all right," Bob said. "We really do seem to be a lot more relaxed when we're together."

"So, you've been taking walks every morning, and you did the dishes together Friday night. Do you think that is enough or do you believe you should be doing other activities together?"

"I just don't think we can," Betty said. "We don't seem to have much time together in the evening, and I'm so tired at the end of the day that I'm just too exhausted."

"Me too," Bob agreed. "From the moment I leave for work till I get home, I don't have a moment's rest. If you work at Willard, you need roller skates because you're just running from one crisis to the next. I use up what little energy is left fighting traffic on the way home. When I walk into the house, I'm exhausted. That's why we both decided to take a walk in the morning."

"Betty, does that sound familiar to you," I asked.

"Well, yes, it's the same way with me. The bank business isn't the way it used to be, that's for sure. What with out-of-state banks coming into Arizona and new computer applications, things have really changed. Our computers deliver greater customer service, but, my God, you wouldn't believe the problems when something goes wrong! My job now involves getting out and developing new market areas while trying to stay on top of everything going on in our branch. When I walk into the house at night, sometimes I just want to go to bed. When Bob was talking about the reduction in stress, he was right, but that is only the stress between us. The stress from work is the same as always."

"That's true for me, too," Bob added. "As I said last week, there are a lot of problems at the plant. The pressures from the boss. The effects on quality by rushing manufacturing when we are trying to meet our end-of-the-month delivery goals. Not to mention the total incompetence of some of my people. As I said, I need roller skates!"

"Now you're both describing a conflict between the amount of time you have at work and the number of demands on that time. Sounds like you're trying to resolve the conflict by overworking your systems. Let's see if we can address this. What do both of you do for lunch?"

"What do you mean by *overworking our systems?*" Bob asked.

"Do you see that cord from the lamp plugged into the electric socket in the wall?" They both nodded. "How many light fixtures and small appliances could I run from that one outlet?" I asked.

"It would depend how much electric current they would each draw," Bob said.

"What will happen when I exceed the capacity of that outlet?"

"You'll blow a fuse," Betty answered.

"And that's what people do when they exceed their capacity to deal with the variety of things they want to accomplish in any given time. The other day I had a woman who is very active within the community visit me concerning the feelings of stress she was experiencing. I'll call her Mary Ann.

"I soon discovered that Mary Ann had no real conflict in her life. She was widowed, but quite content living alone with several of her children and grandchildren nearby. She was financially secure and had many friends, including several very close friendships.

"Since there seemed to be no apparent incompatible conflicts, I looked for the other kind of conflict – that is, the kind that results from trying to satisfy a goal over which we have no control or too many goals at once. I asked Mary Ann to list all the things that were important to her, including those areas in which she was active. I instructed her to make one list that contained all the things she tried to accomplish each and every day and another list of those things she tried to accomplish less often.

"Mary Ann came up with a list twenty-five items long, most of which needed her time on a daily basis. I then had her evaluate each item as to its relative importance to her other activities. Once she set her priorities, she began by eliminating the five lowest items on her list. In her case, she was only physically able to deal with so many items. When she went beyond that number, her system began to break down. In other words, it wasn't the goal itself she couldn't accomplish. She simply kept running out of time. In fact, that very day when she went home, she resigned her position as an officer in four different organizations.

I saw Mary Ann the following week and, needless to say, she was a much happier and more relaxed person. She had realized that her system was designed to produce a limited amount of energy and could only do so much."

"But everything I do is necessary," Betty pleaded.

"Well, let's take a look at what you do, and you decide," I said. She looked doubtful, so I smiled and added, "Or do you want to commit yourself to continual stress and exhaustion?"

"No way," she said, smiling nervously.

"Sometimes, Betty – unlike Mary Ann's situation – everything we do is necessary. But there are ways we can pick up some relaxation time. We can do what we have to do in less time by getting someone else to help us or by being more efficient. Or we can simply eliminate part of what we think we need to do. Also, we can reduce our vision of what has to be done to a point below the maximum we believe we can tolerate. If, as a manager, I think of all the things I have to do for the day, it could be overwhelming. If I only look at what the next hour demands, I've reduced my perception of required tasks by seven-eighths. It isn't the tasks that confront me, but my conscious reflection of them when I compare them to what I perceive as too much. Let's review a typical day in your life, such as yesterday."

"Well, Bob and I got up at six, and were walking by six fifteen," she began. "We returned to the house at seven, and I went in Ruthie's room to make sure she was up. Then to the kitchen to fix breakfast for Tim and Ruthie. Then I showered and got dressed for work. When I went back into the kitchen, the children had nearly finished eating. I drank some orange juice as I cleaned up the dishes, then I was off to the bank.

"When I came home from the bank it was about five thirty. I changed clothes, then headed for the kitchen. I had planned to have dinner at six, but Bob called and said he would be a half hour late. So we ate when he got home at six thirty. Then Bob and I cleaned up the kitchen. I helped Ruthie finish her homework and played cards with her till her bedtime. Then I read for a while and went to bed around ten."

"What did you do for lunch?" I asked her.

"We have a room at the bank where we eat lunch. I took some reports I had to read and then half way through lunch, one of my employees came into the lunchroom to discuss some customer problems with me."

"Is that typical of how you spend your lunch break?"

"Why, yes, I guess it is," she replied.

"Do you remember the other day when I was talking with you about reorganization? You mentioned that sometimes when you try to write a report you have difficulty thinking through what you want to say. And you told me how you handled that problem."

"I know exactly what I do," she replied. "I get up from my desk, leave my office, walk around the branch for a while, and ultimately something comes to me. I return to my office and finish the report. It works every time."

"That method allows you to let reorganization happen in a relaxed state, without putting any other demands on your system. Do you also remember when we talked about feelings, and I mentioned how we increase the amount of energy within our system – sometimes very hostile energy – without safely using it up?"

"Yes, I do," she responded.

"Most of this energy is usually generated by the many things during the day that we are unable to resolve or control. A safe way to use up this energy is to get away from those areas that we are having difficulty controlling and to rest. Or, as an alternative, we can do something that uses up the hostile energy while resupplying our system with the good feelings generated by successful, relaxing activities."

"What you're trying to tell me is that working during my lunch hour isn't a great idea, is that it?" she said, grinning.

"Nothing like coming right to the point. You put your system under pressure all morning, and you just don't let up over the noon hour. I guess, when you became a manager running your own show, working through the lunch hour became a permanent part of how you perceived your new position."

"That's true during my lunch breaks, too," Bob said. "I'll be in a meeting, and they bring in the food. Or I'm on the run from one crisis to another. Or I'm settling an individual problem with one of my people. Sometimes I get so busy I don't have time to eat."

"Is the kind of lunch break you're taking helping you get what you want – relief from the stress you're generating in your daily life?"

"Obviously not," Betty said. "But I don't like going out to eat. It just seems to take up so much valuable time, and it gets expensive."

"Who says you have to eat during your entire lunch break?" I asked.

"What do you mean?" Bob asked.

"I have a friend who manages numerous plants for a high tech manufacturing company. He has an extremely bright mind, a delightful sense of humor, and he runs a very tight ship. Harry has over 5,000 employees under him, and he's highly sensitive to the quality and on-time delivery of his products. At noon, he eats a few pieces of fruit for lunch. This takes him all of five minutes. You'd never guess what he does for the rest of his lunch hour. He picks up the trash in the company parking lot, around the bushes, and on the lawn that surrounds the area where his company is located."

"You've got to be kidding?" Bob said, laughing.

"Harry claims that it takes him away from his work long enough to get him relaxed. A side benefit is that, besides getting a little exercise, he has the cleanest plant in the corporation, and you can guess why!"

Bob nodded. "I can imagine the ground crews are constantly on their toes with the plant superintendent out doing some of their work every noon. Seriously, though, it does make sense to get away from the phones, office interruptions, and all the things that go on in a manufacturing plant."

Betty thought for a minute. "I never thought of it before, but taking a walk at noon would get me away from the phones and other disturbances during lunch, and give me a chance to regain some composure. It might even put me in a better mood during the afternoon. I don't want to pick up trash though," she added with a grin.

"A physician who came to see me several months ago was suffering all kinds of stress, especially during the evening hours with her husband. She arrived at the hospital at seven thirty every morning and was there until five or six at night. She usually attended meetings over the noon hour, and never had a relaxing lunch. Part of her new plan was to take a walk every noon. She would leave the hospital, walk in one direction, and turn around only after she had felt the tension of the morning gone.

"My son, John, has a growing business in California and has offered all his employees a free spa membership if they take advantage of it at least three times a week during their lunchbreak. The activity consumes the hostile energy that develops during the morning hours in a safe, healthy way and allows for a more productive, relaxed afternoon.

"A friend of mine plays poker with four friends over the noon hour, and a recent client began a noon hour backgammon tournament at his office. This relaxing over the noon hour does make a difference. I have a good friend, Doug, who has a large family, so he does his relaxing time in the library on the way home."

"You know, there are these two maintenance foreman in their sixties who play chess every noon at work," Bob said. "I've often wondered what keeps them so sane, what with all the pressures they're under. Now I know."

"How about when you leave work, can either of you apply the same idea to that time?" I asked.

"When I leave work, I fight the traffic home," Bob said. " When I walk into the house, I must admit that I'm not in the best of moods." Betty looked at Bob and nodded.

"Can you possibly fit some relaxation time between when you leave work and the time when you integrate with your family?" I asked.

"A few of the women at work have been after me to join them at a health spa right after work," Betty said. "The problem is that I'm needed at home."

"What time would you get home if you joined the health spa?"

"Oh, probably forty-five minutes to an hour later than I usually do," Betty replied. She paused, thought for a moment, then continued. "You know, it might not be a bad idea to try that out. I know I'd feel better, and Ruthie is generally playing or doing her homework with her friend, Sally Ann, next door. I could check with Sally Ann's mother to see if she would mind watching her for that extra time. I'm sure she wouldn't mind."

"After I get home I could escape to the bedroom and take a twenty-minute nap, or I could even take a short bike ride with Ruthie if she's home," Bob responded. "She's always wanting to do something."

"Do you think these ideas will help?"

"Oh, I'm sure they would help me," Betty replied. "I feel so tense when I get home. It seems that all I'm looking forward to is bed. I don't think that's the kind of attitude I should have when surrounded by my family."

"I know it will help me," Bob said. "I've found myself far more relaxed driving to work since we began our morning walks. I'm sure it will do us both some good. Before coming to see you, we were both pretty upset most of the time. Things are certainly better than they were, but how do you deal with someone who is really upset, or, worse yet, who gets moody, you know, won't talk to you, someone who just wants to be left alone?"

"Leave her alone."

"Thank you, Ed," Betty said quietly, looking at her husband.

"I don't get it," Bob said. "Why do you say 'leave her alone'? "

"Bob, tell me about the last time you had this problem with Betty," I said, looking directly at him.

"Last week, Betty was so angry! And yet I hadn't done anything that I could see," he began, his voice rising a little defensively. "I tried to talk with her, you know, to help her deal with her problem, tried to understand her, to find out why she was so upset. The more I tried, the worse it got."

"What is it that you wanted?"

"Well, I don't know," he stammered. "I guess I wanted her to calm down, so we could talk, work things out."

"What is it that you wanted that you thought working things out would accomplish?" I continued.

"Gosh, I guess I wanted things to be better between us," he said. "I wanted her to give me some attention."

"Did trying to talk with her get you what you wanted?".

"Well, no, of course not," he responded. "Things only got worse."

"He even got so mad he slammed the bedroom door shut and then slammed the front door shut," Betty added.

"Did slamming the doors help?" I asked.

Bob looked embarrassed. "Of course not. None of that worked. Yet, why wouldn't talking with her help? Isn't that what you're supposed to do, talk things out when you're upset? I didn't slam doors until after she refused to talk about whatever upset her in the first place."

"Bob, when was the last time you were upset about something yourself?"

"Today," he said. "I was trying to resolve a problem between engineering and production to enhance the quality of one of our most popular products. I was so angry at everyone that I just went into my office, closed the door, and tried to cool down. That's when Julie – the boss' ear, you know, Miss Personnel herself – comes in. She saw I was mad and tried to find out what was wrong, and the more she pried, the madder I got and. . ." Bob became very quiet, looked down for a moment, then looking at me, he continued slowly, "I think I see what you mean."

"Often, Bob, when people get upset, their feelings only reflect some kind of internal conflict they're experiencing. That's true no matter what they're feeling – whether they're angry or depressed, confused or anxious. That sense of discomfort is what I talked about earlier and is a sign of. . ."

"Reorganization," Betty said, interrupting.

I nodded. "That's right, Betty. When people are in conflict, they often tend to ignore others. They tend to isolate themselves in an attempt to reorganize, that is, to deal with their own internal worlds. A client I've been seeing has been trying to deal with his moods of depression by either taking a walk or just isolating himself from his family by going into his bedroom so as not to cast a gloomy atmosphere within his home. The problem he's been having is that his wife has perceived his actions as a rejection of her when he's just trying desperately to deal with his own internal world. The poor man is trying to improve himself and has really been improving, but now his wife refuses to work at the marriage. She said, 'I'm not just going through any more of his rejecting moods.' What he needed was acceptance. He wasn't rejecting his wife. He was just trying to find some time alone to reconcile his own discomfort. Fortunately, she's recently recognized her misunderstanding of her husband's actions, and their marriage is back on track."

"Just remember, never push on an internal control system, especially when it's trying to deal with itself. Your action will only result in more violence within the system. For a system to deal effectively when it feels the discomfort of a problem, it has to deal with itself. That's the way it's designed. **When a control system is upset, leave it alone.** It's struggling with a world you know nothing about – trying desperately to re-establish harmony within and between its various levels. It may be trying to resolve differences in its value system or re-evaluating its whole system of priorities. It might be trying to compare its standards with the actions it has been taking.

"Meanwhile, it's having to deal with the feelings of discomfort, whether they be sensed as stress or anxiety, depression or guilt, anger or frustration. Who knows? It's being bombarded with all sorts of perceptions from the reorganization system, which it's having to sort out and think through. In short, it's got lots of things it's trying to deal with and it's very busy right then.

"Then along comes another person – controlling for something, trying to pry into an area it knows nothing about, not having the vaguest idea of the problems that are being dealt with internally. This person is trying to find out what is going on in a vain attempt to offer what is thought to be wise advice. Now the person whose control system is in conflict has another problem – an interfering outsider offering well-intentioned advice but whose presence is, at best, unwelcome.

"When problems arise, people usually need time alone not only to reduce the hostile feelings that build up during the day as a result of unresolved desires, but also just to deal with and resolve internally their own conflicts. It is during this time alone, without the noise and demands of the world impinging on us, that most people find it easiest to bring their own world back into balance. If people need help, let them ask for it. **Never try to force your world on another.** It will only result in more chaos."

"I thought Betty was trying to ignore me, and I felt hurt," Bob protested.

"You felt hurt because you wanted Betty to love you and be nice to you. You perceived Betty was in an angry mood, and you weren't getting what you wanted. So you were trying to change her to the way you wanted her to be. As you admitted minutes ago, it didn't work."

"So, as I was trying to deal with my own world, Bob thought I was intentionally trying to get rid of him," Betty said thoughtfully. "He perceived I was rejecting him, the same as your client."

"Right, Bob perceived you as not caring about him. When people isolate themselves or when they're angry, they must be left alone to deal with their own worlds. That's the most efficient way to reorganize."

"What do you mean?" Bob asked.

"When people are in conflict, they need a calm, accepting atmosphere in which to work out their problems. In Betty's case, once she had calmed down and had resolved the difficulty she was having, she probably would have been a lot different to deal with. It is that accepting atmosphere that others can offer those who are in conflict that is so important. Trying to deal with our worlds, whether we feel anger or depression or whatever, is tough enough, without critical interference from others.

"I recently had a young couple in here for counseling. Every morning the woman had been waking up angry, banging things around while making a lot of nasty remarks. Her husband tried to grab her, and, when he caught her, he would shake her. She was going to leave him because on top of her other conflicts, she perceived her husband as violent. Once he learned to leave her alone, to keep from criticizing her, and to remain calm and loving, she began to give up the rather bizarre behavior. Obviously, at the same time I helped her work through several conflicts with which she was trying to deal."

"I never thought about just leaving Betty alone," Bob said, shaking his head. "I really wanted to help her, and she wouldn't let me, so I found myself making things worse. That made me angry."

"There are three rules to remember here. First, never push on another control system, telling it what to do, especially when it is trying to deal with an internal problem. The second rule is, if you want to know what is going on, ask if you can help. If you find you're not wanted, stay away. Third, accept human beings with their individual control systems, struggling to deal with themselves. People need acceptance more than they need advice. That is what a loving relationship is all about. When I'm upset, Hester just leaves me alone and waits for me to calm down. I know she cares, and I appreciate her acceptance of me."

"How do you know she cares?" Bob asked.

"First, we have had a close, on-going, loving relationship for many years. Second, we both understand that leaving each other alone when we're upset is a caring thing to do. If we need help, we'll ask for it."

"Makes sense," Bob observed.

"Getting back to alone time, there is one more benefit that comes to mind. There are times when being alone allows us to find extreme pleasure in some kind of satisfying routine. I personally enjoy writing, especially when I watch my mind exploding with new ideas and new ways of looking at old ones. This is something that brings sheer pleasure to my life and, as a result, makes the rest of my day more satisfying. Also, I find this same experience when I lecture or teach. As I give my presentation or help someone learn the skills of working with others, I find ideas bouncing out of my mind. It's all highly pleasurable. Do either of you have any special activity that provides you with pleasure like that?"

Bob sighed. "Years ago, I used to play the piano, but I've gotten so busy over the years that I never play anymore."

"Were you skilled enough that you could just sit down and enjoy the music as you played?" I asked.

"Oh, yes," Bob said. "My mother claimed I would 'space out'. She would call me several times before I would answer. Betty had the same problem with me when we were first married, but then the children came along, and I got away from it. I used to really love it, though."

"Do you think it helped you relax?"

"Absolutely!" he said with feeling. "It was very relaxing."

"How are you spending your evenings now?"

"I know, glued to the television set," Bob said disgustedly. "You know, I never thought of that. I use to love playing music. We still have that old piano, but it probably needs tuning. I'll test it out tonight."

"How about playing at least half an hour every day for a week?" I suggested.

"You've got it," Bob said enthusiastically.

"Betty, let's take a look at the list of things you do everyday that are good," I suggested. Betty handed me her list.

Good Things - Betty

Monday:	1. cooked dinner 2. put Ruthie to bed
Tuesday:	1. went to work 2. left work on time
Wednesday:	1. read reports 2. took client to lunch
Thursday:	1. 2.
Friday:	1. played cards with Ruthie 2. stayed on diet
Saturday:	1. walked with Bob 2. called Mom
Sunday:	1. 2.

"Have you noticed anything in trying to keep this list?" I asked.

Betty showed some concern. "I'm running out of things to put down on my list."

"That's the benefit of getting very specific. What does putting Ruthie to bed entail?"

"Oh, brushing her hair, reading to her, helping her clean up her room and getting her clothes out for school." Betty was silent for a minute, then added, "I can see what you mean, I've been a little general in my comments."

"Now that you understand what I mean by getting specific, what have you found happening to yourself as you have been thinking about what you have done?"

"At first I felt funny, like it really wasn't me that I was talking about, that I was being phony," Betty replied. "I also felt like 'So what?' I'm

supposed to do all this stuff. In addition, after the first two days, I had a hard time thinking of anything I was doing that was good. It was a very strange experience."

"Do you understand why you're doing this?"

"I guess so," she replied, not quite convinced.

"Remember, when we build our worlds into our perceptual systems we begin to adopt ways of thinking and acting that seem to work best in dealing with our environments. As we repeat these actions, we set patterns for accomplishing various tasks. As babies begin to feed themselves, their use of utensils is awkward, and they often miss their mark by a wide margin as they attempt to get food into their mouths. Ultimately, as we develop, we learn the patterned behavior of feeding ourselves so that we don't even think of what we have to do. We just do it. The thought we have is that 'I want to eat.' Then we perceive the food, and our system does it's job without our having to think of any of our exact muscle movements.

"Bob, when you described playing the piano, I'm sure you don't think about which keys your hands are hitting. You just listen to the feedback, which is the sound of the music." Bob nodded vigorously .

"Well, Betty." I continued. "We not only set patterns for our physical activities such as eating, brushing our teeth, getting undressed, or playing the piano, but we also develop patterns for the way we perceive our environments and ourselves. Many people create, at program level, a way of thinking about themselves as inferior and incompetent. All the things they imagine indicate that they will never make it. Ultimately, this becomes a habit, and they never really view themselves as having made the choices to get where they are or think the way they do. But they really have constructed the way they think. As one of you said before, you think it's part of your nature, when – in reality – you designed the habit yourself.

"All you're doing through this exercise is trying to develop a different way of looking at yourself. You're forcing yourself to look at and evaluate the good things you do by writing two new good things you see yourself doing each day. You're feeding back into yourself a different perception than what you have created about yourself in the past. That's why you sense it as strange. You're not used to it. Once you've developed this new way of looking at yourself, you will eventually develop it into a habit and continue to look at yourself and your day-to-day accomplishments in a new, positive way."

"I see what you mean," Betty said.

Bob shook his head. "I never realized that about you, Betty. I would never have guessed. I've heard you criticize others, but I never noticed that you did that to yourself. But my problem is different than yours. I'm a worrier. I've been that way all my life. I just can't help it."

"Did you hear what you just said, Bob?"

"I don't think I can help it, Ed."

"Does the idea of a patterned way of looking at things make sense to you?" I asked him.

"Yes, I guess so." Bob thought for a minute, then asked, "Do you really think we design it that way and create the habit ourselves?"

"How else would it get to be that way? It's your brain that's doing it. Who do you think created all those various ways of thinking and acting within you?"

"Well, I know I create my own perceptions, but I never thought that worry is a result of how I perceive things," he said. "Are you suggesting that I could develop a way to look at things so I wouldn't worry?"

"If these ideas work for Betty, why shouldn't they work for you?"

"I guess they should," he replied. "So do I keep a list or what?"

"Try writing down two things that happen every day that are good, and you're not allowed to repeat anything once you've written it down. People who worry create perceptions of future events turning out poorly. What I want you to do is to identify events that turn out well.

"For example, your boss says something nice to you or your monthly production forecast is on target. These are good things. Betty shows you some affection, Tim greets you in the morning, Julie calls from school and doesn't ask for money. Your car starts on the first try, you don't need work on your teeth, a tree you planted didn't die in the summer heat. There are just lots of good things that happen to us every day. Just give it a try, and, remember, you can't repeat anything once you have written it down."

"OK, I'll give it a try. I'll really give it a try," Bob said, grinning.

Betty began to smile and said, "I just thought of something. What if both of us walk into the house at the same time, and we're both up tight. Dinner or one of the children has to be attended to. Who gets to have their alone time first?"

"I once had a couple give me the solution to that very problem," I said, smiling. "They would tell each other where their tension level was on a scale of one to ten. Whoever had the lowest on the scale would attend to the immediate domestic requirements. If there was a tie, then they took turns.

"Well, our time is up for today, but, before you leave, I'd like each of you to tell me what your plan is for this coming week."

Bob was the first to speak. "I'm going to make a list of two things that happen every day that are good. Betty and I will keep doing our quality time together. Also, I think I'll go for a walk over the noon hour at work, and I'll spend at least fifteen minutes on the piano every night."

Betty spoke next. "I'm going to continue to keep my lists, and I think I'll join my friends after work at the spa. It should help me with my weight problem as well. At noon I think I'll get out and take a walk. I like that idea. The summer heat in Arizona can get to you, so I think I'll go to a nearby mall. It's cool inside, and I can set a nice brisk pace."

I also asked Betty and Bob to review how they spent their mornings from the time they finished their walk until they left the house for work. I was curious to see whether they would be able to reduce the things they 'needed to do.'

We made an appointment for the following week.

Chapter 9

LEARNING TO DEAL WITH OTHERS

The following week, I found my clients waiting for me. "Betty, Bob, it's good to see the two of you. How have you been getting along?" Betty smiled. "Much better, Ed, we're getting along much better." "Things between us have really improved," Bob agreed. "It's hard to believe it happened so quickly."

"Bob, what changes have you noticed in Betty?"

"Well, she wasn't upset the other night when I came home late without calling. The minute I walked in, she got up from reading the paper and fixed my dinner. She sat and chatted with me while I ate. She's been more attentive to me and more relaxed. She's been letting the kids fix their own breakfasts in the morning so we would have a little more time on our walks. That way we aren't so rushed."

"Betty, are you aware of what Bob is saying about you?"

"No, I hadn't thought of it until he mentioned it. He certainly is becoming more considerate. He's been doing little things around the house without my asking – things I have been nagging him to do for years. Over the weekend he fixed the window in Ruthie's room. Its been cracked for years."

"Have you both been keeping your lists?"

"It does make a difference," Betty said. "Keeping the list, that is. It's strange how it happens, how my thinking has changed. It's funny how, all of a sudden, I've begun to think of little things, you know, the good things about myself – even though I'm not consciously making the effort to do so. It really does work."

"Did you bring the list of the good things you've been doing?"

"I'm afraid I left it home, but I can assure you that I've gotten very specific on my list," Betty said, laughing. "I put down 'fixed peas and carrots' instead of 'fixed dinner'. It really has become an eye opener. I never realized what it's like to feel so good. It really does work."

"It is still a little strange for me," Bob said. "I guess I haven't been keeping mine long enough. It's hard for me to think of new things that happen every day that are good, It really is. But I'm doing it. I'm afraid I left my list on my nightstand, but Betty and I have been making sure we write only specific items and that we keep our lists current. We've even talked about what we wrote."

"That's fine. Betty, are you doing your noon walk, and how about the spa after work?"

"I've been going three days a week to the spa, and, right now, I'm really sore from it all. But it's been worth it," she said happily. "It's been too hot for walking during lunch and driving to the mall takes too much time. However, I love to read, and our branch has two conference rooms. I use the small one over lunch to get in some pleasure reading. With my hectic schedule, this has really been most relaxing for me."

"Bob, how about you?"

"I've been getting out for a half hour over the noon hour. Even though I wear a hat, it's too hot for a longer walk. It's been helping. What's been really great is playing the piano. The only problem was keeping Ruthie away, but I've started letting her sit quietly by my side, and it works out fine. Very relaxing. I'd forgotten what it was like.

"I think we're beginning to gain some confidence in each other," Bob said, looking seriously at me. "The children are another problem, though. Especially Tim. We've both been spending time with Ruthie, and she seems to be a lot happier, more approachable, you know, easier to handle. Tim still ignores us and does what he wants."

Betty agreed. "I'm afraid that's true, He's very strong willed. Ruthie's teacher sent home a note saying she has noticed an improvement in her attitude and behavior. She has been paying more attention and participates more in class."

"It's been my experience that the happier children are at home, the fewer problems they have at school. What I'd like to do today is to go over another area of stress, the kind that is brought on by the conflicts that develop through having to deal with others – whether your children or people at work. Is that still an important area to both of you?"

They nodded in agreement.

"Bob, do you remember the demonstration with the two rubber bands tied together and your attempt to keep the knot over the dot?"

"I sure do. I even told Betty about it."

"If you remember, I explained how parents, for example, invariably look at what their children are doing and assume from what they see and hear that they understand why their offspring are acting the way they are. I also suggested that what causes another's actions is a combination of the person's perceptions and wants. With that in mind, what do you think is causing your spouse to become more accommodating to you?" Betty spoke up. "Well, as you explained, we deal with our perception of another, not with the actual person. I suppose as I change my perception of Bob and as he begins to improve in my eyes, I change how I treat him."

Bob nodded, but protested, "You know, that's an easy concept to understand when you explain it, but when you see someone doing something you don't like, it's very hard not to get upset. Last night Tim spouted off at Betty, and it was all I could do to keep from yelling at him. I just walked out of the house and went for a walk until I felt better. I didn't want to make things worse, and I just couldn't think of a better way of handling the situation."

"How did you perceive Tim?"

Bob looked at me and then down at the floor. "Do you really want to know?" I nodded my head. "Frankly, I hate to admit this with one of my own kids, but I just can't stand him any more. It seems the more he's around, the more irritating he becomes. I guess that's partially why I'm so stressed out and why I want to learn how to work with that kid."

"Bob, the first day you came to see me, you were very upset and concerned about yourself. Yet, at the end of the session, you seemed to calm down. What was it that I asked you that helped you calm yourself down?"

Bob sat quietly, thinking over what had happened. "I never thought about it, but when I began talking about what was important to me and what I wanted, I guess it gave me something solid to look at and work toward. I also felt you knew what you were talking about."

"Do you think the same approach might be helpful with Tim?"

"What do you mean?" he asked, puzzled.

"The key to dealing with others is to try as much as possible to find out about their worlds. The best place to begin is to find out what they want, just as I did with each of you when you first came to see me. I asked you what was important to you, how you set your priorities, the standards you had set that reflected your values, and the specific decisions you were attempting to make.

"When most people see someone acting in a negative way – such as Tim with his mother last night – their first reaction is to chew that person out, lay out what's right or wrong, and tell the person what to do.

That's not only a highly inefficient way of handling people – it can decrease the ability of people to deal with themselves.

"For example, suppose, Betty, that you came home from the bank after having had numerous frustrations throughout the day. While trying to find a Band-Aid for a cut finger, you found one of your favorite china dishes broken. Bob walks into the kitchen and tells you that you left the front door open and let in some flies. Will Bob's comment make it easier or harder for you to work through your own situation?"

"Obviously, it will make things harder, but shouldn't you correct children – and even adults sometimes – when you see them doing something wrong?"

"I'll ask you. Without knowing what they want and how they perceive things, should you correct children's behavior?"

"I've always thought that was the parent's job," Betty said. "How else are they going to learn?"

"You have two children in their twenties plus two others. As you reflect back over the years with your children, have your lectures and admonishments been effective?"

"I'll answer that with a big 'no'," Bob interrupted. "Most of the time they just don't listen."

"Prior to coming here, did you listen to Betty?"

"You know the answer to that," Bob said, half smiling.

"What I'm trying to get at is this. When people have things on their mind that have a higher priority than what you're telling them, they're not going to give much consideration to what you're saying – no matter how important it is to you. We are designed to always put higher priority items ahead of lower ones. And this all presupposes that you have a good relationship with people and they want to work with you."

"So when I tell Tim to show respect to his mother. . ." Bob began.

"Bob, what do you think was on his mind? What did he want?"

"He probably wanted to get some money for a show or to get quick access to some food so he could spend his usual two hours on the phone talking to his airhead girlfriend," Bob said sarcastically.

"Which, in his mind, was probably at a higher priority than what you or Betty might have wanted."

"So, how do you get through to him?" Bob asked.

"By finding out what he wants. Betty, what happened last evening between you and Tim?"

"Well, Tim came into the kitchen, wanting to know about dinner, saying he was in a hurry. I told him that Bob was working late and that we would be eating around seven. Then Tim became upset, started cursing, saying he wanted to eat now. That's when Bob walked in from the garage."

Bob interjected, "Yeah, I was so pleased at getting away from work on time after all. Then I walked into this mess! I told him not to talk to his mother that way. He just mumbled a few words and went to his room, slamming the door behind him."

"Let me suggest a few ideas you might keep in mind. First, you never want to talk with anyone about a problem when either you or the other person is upset. Once you're both calmed down, then you ask the person – in this case Tim – if he wants to talk with you. If he doesn't, all you can do is wait till he's ready. If you push your children to talk with you before they're ready, as Betty recognized a few minutes ago, things could get a lot worse. You would just be adding to the burden of things they're trying to cope with.

"If you attempt to deal with Tim, for example, I would begin by asking him if he's willing to talk with you. If he says 'no' or makes a smart remark, I wouldn't make any judgement about him or about what he has said. I would just say 'I'll try later' and leave him alone. When he has worked through some of the internal conflict he has going on within him, he will calm down. Once he's more relaxed, I would try again, asking him if he's now willing to talk with you.

"The closer the relationship you have with Tim, the more likely he will want to be reconciled with you. A strong relationship can gradually be built through quality time and will give you the first necessary ingredient needed for dealing with your children. It's the key to relating with colleagues at work – or anyone, for that matter. You need to be perceived by them as sensitive to what's going on in their life before they're willing to open up to you. Spending quality time together helps them create that perception of you. Without that awareness on their part, you stand less chance of establishing a good working relationship with Tim or anyone else."

"Neither of us has spent any time with him, that's for sure," Betty said. "Not that we have really wanted to, for that matter. Now he's so caught up with his friends that I doubt if he would want to spend time with us. He only does chores around the house when he needs money."

"One way to access teen-age children is to work one-on-one together with them, such as doing the dishes or laundry, cleaning up a room, washing a car, or working in the yard. It is a subtle way of building a close relationship without making it as obvious as asking them to play a game. Giving various members of the family individual jobs to do is fine, but doing tasks in pairs allows for building of relationships through quality time alone together."

"Ruthie seems to have responded quite well to biking with Bob and playing games with each of us," Betty said. "Do all younger children react this quickly?"

"That depends on the child. Anytime I have parents come to me with a concern about their pre-teen children, I generally look for four things. First, how much quality time each parent spends alone with them individually. Second, how much play activity time they spend both alone and with other children their own age. Third, how much television they watch. Fourth, how much sugar they're consuming.

"We've already talked about the need for quality time with their parents. Learning to spend time alone with a parent has to then translate into the child's peer relationships, which are critical to a child's development. As for television, it isn't what children watch on television that's so bad, but rather it's the enormous amount of time they spend in front of the set. Children naturally develop their socializing skills through play with others, and they learn to enjoy the use of their own minds through playing by themselves. Prior to television, all this took place within the course of a child's daily life. Watching television takes away from the time needed for this developmental process. That's why so many children have difficulty getting along with their class-mates and learning to obey standards when they go to school. They haven't matured sufficiently to meet the social demands of school."

"That's interesting," Betty remarked. "Our June, who is good at finding things to amuse herself, never did watch TV very much."

"Finally, I find in my own counseling practice and from observing some of my grandchildren that, the higher the sugar intake, the more hyperactive children become. They tend to run around without much direction. I remember a young mother of four children under six who came to see me about how to better handle her children. As she and her husband developed the practice of quality time, they all settled down except one. When I asked about the child's sugar intake, she replied, 'Oh Danny loves sugary things. He even takes his money for school lunch and uses it to buy candy.' Two weeks after she removed all high sugar content substances from the house and pre-paid his school lunch, Danny came home with a 'Best Behaved Student of The Week' award.

"Let's get back to Tim. Once he would be willing to do so, you could try dealing with Tim by getting him to look at what he wanted, how he perceived things, and asking him to make comparisons between what he wanted and how he saw things. Perhaps I could show you what I mean by doing a role play with you. One of you play Tim, and I'll play one of you. Perhaps you can get some ideas that way. We'll play it as though I'm approaching him after he has calmed down."

"I'll try since I'm with him more," Betty said. Bob agreed.

"O.K., Betty, I'll be you, and you'll be Tim. Ready?" Betty nodded.

Betty (played by Ed):   "Tim, are you willing to talk with me?

Tim (played by Betty): "What do you want?"

Betty: "I'd like to talk with you about how we could get along better. Are you interested?"

Tim: "All you want to do is preach to me."

Betty: "Are you willing to talk with me for a few minutes?"

Tim: "Do I have a choice?" There was a slight hesitation. "Yeah, I guess so."

Betty: "Would you like to get along better with Dad and me?"

Tim: "You could just leave me alone, stay off my back, and let me do things with my friends."

Betty: "Would you like to get along better with Dad and me?"

Tim: "I don't know."

Betty: "Are you satisfied with how things are going at home?"

Tim: "No, it sucks."

Betty: "Tim, do you really want to talk now? Should I come back later, or would you rather things stay the way they are?"

Tim: "All right, I'll talk."

Betty: "Would you like to get along better with your Dad and me?"

Tim: "Yeah, I guess so."

Betty: "Are you sure."

Tim: "Yeah, I'm sure."

Betty: "Are you interested in working out a way that Dad and I could get along with you?"

Tim: "Yes, I would like that."

Betty: "Are you satisfied with the rules we've set for you?"

Tim: "I don't think they're fair."

Betty: "What particular rules aren't fair?"

Tim: "I don't think I should have to stay home on school nights, and I should be allowed to stay out until two or so on Friday and Saturday nights. All my friends can."

Betty (played by Ed):   "Are there any other rules that you're con-
            cerned about?"
Tim (played by Betty): "You won't let me get my drivers' permit."
Betty: "Are there any other items?"
Tim: "No, just those."
Betty: "What are the conditions for going out during the middle of
            the week that you think would be fair?"
Tim: "If I do my chores and get my homework done, then I should
            be able to go out if I'm home by eleven or so."
Betty: "Do you think your freedom on a school night should be tied
            to how well you're doing in school?"
Tim: "I don't know."
Betty: "Do you think your father and I should care about how well
            you do in school, or do you think we should ignore it?"
Tim: "I think you should care. It's just boring, that's all."
Betty: "Do you think we do care about you and how well you do in
            school?"
Tim: "Yes."
Betty: "Tim, do you want to graduate from high school?"
Tim: "Sure I do."
Betty: "Do you want to go to college?"
Tim: "Yeah, if I'm accepted."
Betty: "Is being accepted important to you?"
Tim: "Yes, it's very important."
Betty: "Is how you're doing now going to get you into college?"
Tim: "No, I guess not."
Betty: "Would you like to do better in school so you can be assured
            of getting into college?"
Tim: "It's so hard. It takes so much time. Besides, they don't teach
            us anything that's important."
Betty: "Tim, what is more important to you, getting into college or
            going out during the week and staying out late on the
            weekends with your friends?"
Tim: "I really would like to get into college."
Betty: "I'm sure your father and I would agree to negotiating an
            extra hour on Saturday night if we saw an improvement in
            your grade point average. Does that sound fair to you?"
Tim: "Yes, that's fair, but what about a driver's license?"
Betty: "What do you think should be the conditions for you getting
            a drivers license?"

Tim: "Well, I suppose my grades have to be better."
Betty: "Do you think you should pay your share of car insurance?"
Tim: "I don't have a job."
Betty: "Should you pay your share of the car insurance?"
Tim: "I suppose, but that means I have to get a job."
Betty: "That's right. Finally, do you think having a drivers' permit should be tied to how well we're getting along with you and vice versa?"
Tim: "I'll try, Mom, but you have to quit criticizing me all the time, and tell Dad to stop calling me stupid. That hurts."
Betty: "Your Dad and I are going for counseling to learn how to get along with our children more effectively. We plan to work at this as well."

"So what do you think, Betty?" I asked.

"Well I can certainly see a big difference from the way we've been dealing with him, that's for sure. It got to me when you asked me whether I thought my parents should care. And, except for the last statement that you were going for counseling, you never once told me what you thought. Even when I asked you a question, you would turn it around. Ed, how would you have talked with Tim when he came into the kitchen wanting to know when dinner was ready?"

"I would have asked him 'What is it that you want, Tim?' or 'Do you have something you want to do?' Thay's the key to finding out what it was that was driving his system, his main goal at the time. It might have been to get out before seven, or he might have had a friend coming over. I'm sure if you had found out what he was actually wanting – or, to put it in my terms, what his system was actually controlling for – then the outcome would have been different."

"I noticed you ignored me when I made remarks in an attempt to sidetrack you from what you were trying to do," Betty said. "I asked you to leave me alone, stay off my back. You just kept focused by asking the same question in a quiet, non-judgmental way."

"One way to handle those who offer excuses or make remarks intended to keep you from being focused is to repeat the question, ignoring the remarks, as I did with you. Other ways are to say nothing or to react by saying, 'I see.' When there is no reaction or judgment made to what is said, people are more likely to evaluate their own worlds and think over what they have said. If you attack someone, he will probably attack back and will be much less inclined to take responsibility for his own world. And why not? He can now blame you as the problem."

"I can see that finding out what a person wants does make a difference," Bob said. "What if, in the role play, Betty had said, 'I can't help myself' or – more typically – 'I don't know.' How would you have handled that?"

"First let me explain what's happening. When teenagers offer these remarks, it's their way of trying to avoid making a value judgement concerning what they've been doing or to avoid dealing in a specific subject area. When I asked you, Betty, whether you would like to get along better with your Dad and me, and you answered the typical 'I don't know' response, I ignored the answer and asked a question which I thought would be harder for you to resist. I said, 'Are you satisfied with how things are going at home?' I tried to get a value judgement in an area which was less threatening and more acceptable to you.

"To get people to work with you, it's best to try to elicit a value judgement or some kind of opinion in an area they find the least threatening to them. Asking a locked-up teenager if he 'wants to get out of here' will more than likely get a quick 'yes' response. Any kind of positive response helps establish some basis, no matter how minimal, for continued negotiations.

"When people are slamming doors, yelling and screaming, making insulting remarks, or ignoring each other, talking to them about what they're doing at that point is useless. You've got to get them calmed down to access them and establish reasonable and rational communications. Once the storm clouds have passed, then you have them talk about what they want, what the rules are, what they're doing, and then ask for evaluations and commitments. Ultimately, the final step to making a permanent change involves good plan-making, including feedback – but I'm getting ahead of myself. We'll talk about that later."

"How do you apply this at work? That's where I have lots of problems." Bob asked.

"O.K., Bob, I'll work with you on that, but, first, let's talk about the principles of dealing with others. What we've talked about thus far is finding out what the person wants at the various levels, as I have done with both of you. And, both during the Tim role play and with the two of you, I talked about how you and he perceived things – not how I perceived things. I asked Tim during the role play if he thought his parents should care about him and how important schooling was to him, which is finding out about his values.

"The more you find out about another person's world, the more you'll be able to adjust your own thinking accordingly. More important, the people with whom you are dealing will be more apt to judge their own words. Giving people an opportunity to evaluate their own thinking is the best way to get them to adjust it as well.

"For this to happen, it should help to use some criteria that I've developed through my own work in training counselors. First, as a general rule, **ask, don't tell**. **Keep questioning them about their worlds.** Keep them focused on what is important to them. Don't tell a person what you think. That person is then inclined to talk about what you said, avoiding the responsibility hook. Also, talking about what you think does little good because the other person couldn't care less about what is important to you."

"I could see that when you role played Tim with me," Betty said. "Since you didn't bring into the discussion what you were thinking, I became totally centered in my own world, what I wanted, how I perceived things, and my judgements about what was better for me."

"That brings up the next criterion which is to **avoid making any verbal judgements** about what others say, because then they'll tend to deal with your judgements of them rather than evaluating their own worlds. Also, **never try to interact with others when either you or they are upset.** Both people should be relaxed. It's the best kind of atmosphere to promote rational and reasonable conversations.

"**Keep them focused on the issue**, which means you keep the direction of the dialogue in your head. Don't let the other person's answers control the conversation. When Tim mentioned he wanted to stay out till two in the morning and that all his friends did, I didn't pick up on his statement. I stayed with the direction I wanted to go."

"I noticed that when I tried several times to sidetrack you, I couldn't do it," Betty said.

"That's where I have control, namely, through the kinds of questions I ask. **I never ask 'why' when it leads to an excuse**, which, again, will sidetrack the issue at hand. Also, **stay specific and repeat the question when the response does not specifically reflect what is asked.** You'll notice that I did that with you."

"Yes, I noticed that," Betty said, smiling. "I got the feeling that the only way to get you to stop asking the question was to answer it."

Bob asked, "What if, when Betty was playing Tim, she had said she was angry and upset, using that as an excuse for what she was doing. How would you have responded?"

"I would have asked her 'What is it that you want that you aren't getting that is causing you to feel the way you do?' **It's important to connect how people feel to what they want.** Remember, as I mentioned last week, all feelings are caused by what we want. Since feelings in and by themselves cannot be efficiently dealt with, I would have moved her to an area over which she had some control, namely what she wanted. In Tim's case, his anger was caused not by the time his mother was planning dinner, but rather by the fact that he wanted to eat earlier than she had mentioned."

"It's so hard, when you see someone doing something, not to believe that her action is not what's causing you to be upset," Bob said.

"Now we come to the most important part of working with others. **Get them to make an evaluation or comparison concerning the various areas within their worlds.** When we make a value judgement or comparisons of the various things we want and perceive, at that moment we begin to develop a sense of control over our lives and how we feel.

"I'm sure, Bob, that, as you began to evaluate the various ways you perceived Betty, the kind of time you were spending with her, how you established her importance within your value system, and then committed yourself to resolving these issues, was this not the beginning of change within you?"

"To tell you the truth, Ed, I never thought of that until now," Bob said. "I do remember my reaction to looking at my values, especially when you got me to put them in order of importance. I began to perceive things differently. It was as though I had never looked at things that way before. It was uncomfortable, but, as you helped me think through these ideas, especially when you had me setting standards, I felt as though there was a light at the end of my stress tunnel."

"I had the same feeling," Betty added. "It's as though I was stepping back and looking at myself, but it was really my own internal world, as you would say. You really never have told me what to do, rather you just continually asked me to look at my own world and, once you got me to be specific, you asked me to evaluate what I wanted and how I perceived things. You did help me work out a plan, though."

"You can use this same approach on others," I told them. "When people begin to evaluate their own worlds, they stop looking at you, others, or events in their lives as the cause of their problems and begin looking at the incongruities between their own values, priorities, standards, actions, and perceptions. It's the evaluative process of their own worlds that makes this happen. That's where responsibility begins and, assuming the willingness on the part of others, that's how to deal with others."

"I wonder if I could work with my boss on this basis?" Bob said. "He was head of manufacturing before I took over, and, because I decreased costs and increased production and quality control, I'm sure he feels very threatened."

"We can try role playing your boss, but let me first finish with my explanation of the steps for using these ideas with others.

"We can make value judgements of the perceptions we've created of others, ourselves, of situations or problems, of our actions, our values, priorities, standards, and even of the alternative choices we have. We can compare what we are doing with what we want and make a judgement, or we may discern that what we are doing is conflicting with something else we want."

"What's that mean?" Bob asked.

"Well, supposing you yell at Tim to stop cursing at his mother, and he does, in fact, stop. What you did accomplished what you wanted. However, if you also wanted to establish a better relationship with Tim, did your action help you grow closer to Tim?"

"No, it sure didn't," Bob said, waving his hand.

"Sometimes you can't get what you want," Betty suggested.

"That's right, Betty, and that's another evaluation. As I mentioned several weeks ago, when you don't have control over getting what you want, you then have to search for an alternative pathway to achieve it.

"Once they're convinced that what they're doing isn't helping them get what they want, **ask if they're willing to work at resolving their conflict. Get them to make a commitment.** The stronger the commitment, the more likely things will get better. In my first session with each of you, I asked if you were willing to commit to working at what you perceived as a needed improvement or at resolving your various conflicts. And if you will both recall, I didn't accept a weak commitment. I had to be sure you really wanted to make the effort. After people make good solid evaluations and commitments, then you **teach people how to make a plan.**"

"Shouldn't they make their own plans?" Bob asked. "It's their worlds."

"Not necessarily. Getting people to examine their worlds, make evaluations and commitments, this is all their responsibility. Plan-making is a learned skill, and this is where others can help. In effect,

once you both committed yourselves to working at the various areas in
your lives to reduce stress, you were then open to my instruction and
help. My job was to teach you how to develop various plans that are
effective in reducing stress. That's part of my expertise. Plan-making
is something we'll go into another day, right now I'd like to help you
with your boss, Bob. I'll play you and you play your boss and let's
suppose I approach you in your office when I know there will be no
disturbances. What's your supervisor's name?"

"Art," Bob replied.

"Now don't be afraid to act toward me as Art treats you."

"I won't," Bob said, smiling.

Bob (played by Ed):   "Art, I wonder if you have a few minutes? I
                        would like to talk with you about my performance."

Art (played by Bob):   "What do you want now, Bob?"

Bob: "Are you interested in talking with me now about my perform-
         ance or would you rather I come back another time?"

Art: "No, now is as good a time as any, I suppose."

Bob: "I could come back if you would find it more convenient."

Art: "No, it's all right. What's on your mind?"

Bob: "I would like to know those areas of my work that you find
         satisfactory and those areas where you believe I'm not meas-
         uring up to your standards."

Art: "I've told you a hundred times what you're doing wrong. The
         production quotas on the K31 are not meeting the marketing
         forecasts, and the quality of the K28 is not meeting standards.
         I know engineering got their design changes screwed up, but
         you're manufacturing manager, and it's your responsibility."

Bob: "Art, is there any area of my performance with which you're
         satisfied?"

Art: "Well, yes, I guess so. I mean, there have been some minor
         improvements in your overall on-time delivery. They're a little
         better."

Bob: "Is there any other area in which you find I am doing well?"

Art: "Well, you did get the 791 produced with less than a one
         percent rejection. That's a fair improvement."

Bob: "Concerning areas in which you believe I need to improve,
         would you identify the most important?"

Art: "Sure, that's easy. You're not satisfying marketing forecasts,
         that's a big one."

Bob: "Having had this job ahead of me, do you have any specific suggestions on how I might improve?"

Art: "Look, Bob, I'm not going to baby-sit you through this job. If you can't figure things out, we'll have to start looking around."

Bob: "Art, what are your standards for the kind of person that should be doing my job?"

Art: "What do you mean, standards? I just expect you to produce, that's all."

Bob: "Do you think it is up to me as a manager to work with my people until they can do their job well?"

Art: "Of course, that's the job of a supervisor."

Bob: "Is it possible for us to work together on the same basis, with you as my manager, so I can learn how to do my job well?"

Art: "That's different. You were appointed to your job by my predecessor because he thought you were the best supervisor he had. You've done a few things well, but you have a lot to learn, and I'm trying to get you up to speed."

Bob: "Art, what kind of standards are the best to use for getting someone like me up to speed, as you say?"

Art: "What are you talking about?"

Bob: "Well, should we be meeting regularly, and discussing specific goals. Is there any particular training I need? Is there a way for me to understand exactly how you presently perceive me and, more important, for me to understand precisely what you want from me? You just mentioned that the job of supervisors was to work with their people. I'm just asking you on what basis should we be working things out?"

Art: "Look, you're at a high enough level in this organization that you shouldn't need this kind of baby-sitting."

Bob: "Are you saying we shouldn't be working more closely together to improve our production figures?"

Art: "Well, no, I'm not saying that. Don't be putting words into my mouth, Bob."

Bob: "Art, are you satisfied with our working arrangement?"

Art: "Well, not exactly. It could be better."

Bob: "Would you like to work with me so that we can improve the overall performance of this facility?"

Art: "O.K., fine, yes, I would."

Bob: "What kind of standards do you think we ought to set to maximize our efficiency in working with each other?"

Art: "Maybe we could meet more often."
Bob: "Fine, how about once a day? I could go over how we're doing,
          perhaps review my chart showing how daily production is
          keeping up with projected goals, our rejection rate, and other
          items you might find important. Would tomorrow at nine, right
          after my production meeting, be a good time?"
Art: "That's fine, Bob, I'll meet with you tomorrow."

"That certainly is a different approach from the one I have been using,"
Bob said. "Also, I noticed how you kept me focused with your
questions, and you wouldn't let me get you off the subject. It was really
hard for me to stay irritable, even though I tried. Why was that?"

"I stayed in your world, respected your answers, didn't argue with
them, continually asked questions, made no verbal judgements concerning your ideas, and I acted as if I was trying to get help in
understanding your position. I just honestly wanted to know how we
could work together to achieve the company's goals."

"I must say, it was interesting watching you work with Bob," Betty
said, "especially from my vantage point as a bank manager. I guess our
problems at work aren't really that different after all."

"We're all trying to deal with one another as human beings, no
matter what the setting. Well, I guess our time is up for today. Here are
a couple of counseling cards to help you remember some of the ideas
I have talked about. I use them to train counselors at the School of Social
Work where I teach. They may help you handle the various people with
whom you have to work."

"When do you want to see us next?" Bob asked.

"I'd like to see you two weeks from today, if that fits in with your
schedules," I said, looking at both of them.

"It does with mine," Bob said. Betty agreed as well.

"See you in two weeks," I said, "and just continue working on what
you have been doing."

COUNSELING
based on control theory
Edward E. Ford, M.S.W.

The more your clients perceive you as someone they trust and who cares about them, the more effective will be your ability to assist them.

1. Exploration – Ask them about their own world.
– what they want, especially at systems concept, principles, program levels
- their perception of themselves, others, their counselor, problems, standards, priorities, what their counselor or others want and perceive and, specifically, their present actions.
As a general rule, ask, don't tell – keep them dealing with their own world, make no verbal judgements; maintain relaxed calm atmosphere; keep them focused; keep direction of the therapy in your head, not in the answers of your client; don't ask why when it leads to an excuse; move from abstract to specific questions; connect feelings to something they want(What is it that you want that you are not getting that is causing you to feel the way you do?); repeat questions if client doesn't answer it; ask one question at a time.

2. EVALUATION – Ask them to make judgement or comparison of:
– the perception they have created of others, of themselves, or of the situation or problem.
– their perception of what they've been doing. Do these actions conflict with principles, standards, systems concepts in their world?
– whether their action is getting them what they presently want. Compare feedback, not just action, with want.
– whether their action is in conflict with other wants they may have, even if it is getting them what they presently want. These comparisons of other wants should be made at the program, principles, and systems concepts levels.
– priorities, especially at systems concepts level, and **standards** at principles level.
– alternative choices at program, principles, and systems concepts levels after reviewing the down-the-road consequences of decisions they perceive open to them.

3. COMMITMENT – Ask if they're willing to commit to working at what they perceive as a needed improvement or at resolving their conflict. Never allow weak commitments – "I'll try" or "If you say so." Since steps two and three are at the heart of getting others to take responsibility for their own life, make sure your are clear in your own mind whether they have properly done Step Two and that there is a strong enough commitment before proceeding to a plan.

4. PLAN – Teach them how to develop a plan to resolve their difficulties. The following are the elements of good plan making:
– take notes – stay focused – do plan – begin it soon – be specific – within client's ability to succeed – measurable goal chart – get client to review & evaluate – counselor & client involved in and commited to plan – client keeps daily written record – client summariazes plan

Chapter 10

SETTING STANDARDS
AT HOME AND AT WORK

We met again two weeks later. "Betty, Bob, it's good to see you again! How have things been going?"

Betty smiled. "Well, a lot has happened, Ed. I guess you might say that Bob and I have found each other again. It's not that our marriage is perfect, but we have come a long way over this past month. The tension between us is mostly gone. We're just so much happier together. It's hard to believe how quickly this has all happened."

"Here's our quality time list, Ed," Bob said. "We didn't miss a single day in two weeks. We had to take a walk at eleven one evening. Betty had gone out to dinner with the women she's been exercising with after work. She called when she was leaving the restaurant and reminded me we hadn't been together all day. I had gone to bed. But I got up, and I was ready to go by the time she was home." They both laughed.

"Are you both keeping your individual lists on improving your self-perception?"

"Well, yes, I am, but that's something else I was going to mention," Betty said. "Jean, my secretary, and several other of my employees at the bank have remarked on how I've changed. When I asked them how, they've all said basically the same thing – that I seem much happier. Jean remarked how I have been less uptight and more relaxed. I'm still going three days a week to exercise classes at the spa. Strangely enough, I weighed myself this morning and found that I had lost four pounds. I know it isn't just the exercise. I really haven't done that much. I just can't understand the sudden weight loss."

"I told you that you were looking better, didn't I?" Bob said, looking at Betty. "You thought I was kidding, but I really meant it."

"Do you remember the rubber band demonstration?" I asked. They both nodded. "Well, Betty, you're not only happier with Bob, which has pretty much reduced one conflict for both of you, but you also have started exercising and spending time reading every noon. Apparently you're working quite hard at keeping your list of positive things you do every day, and this has begun to change the way you perceive yourself."

"In the rubber band experiment, I showed you how we consciously deal with our perceptions and what we want and that we're generally unaware of what we do. Any time we want something, the thing or person we're trying to control or change is called a *variable*. The variable is what our mind is focused on or what we're trying to change. If you take a look at the left side of this chart, you'll see three boxes labeled *disturbances, variable,* and *actions*. Using the rubber experiment, which box would represent the knot over the dot?"

"It would be the *variable* box," Betty said, "since you're trying to control the relationship of the knot to the dot."

"That's right, Betty. Now, how about the other boxes, what would they represent?"

"Well, obviously, my movements would go in front of the *actions* box," Bob said, "and your movements, Ed, would be in front of the *disturbances* box." Bob was quiet for a moment, then continued, "This helps me understand what you meant when you said that we really aren't that conscious of what we do. Our *actions* are just our attempt to manipulate things we're trying to control – or the *variable,* as you call it, to get what we want."

"Remember my example of wanting to drive forty-five miles-an-hour? What would each of those boxes represent in that example?"

"Well, the *variable* would be the speedometer," Bob responded, "and my *actions* would be my foot on the accelerator."

"And a slow driver in front would be a *disturbance,*" Betty added.

"Now let's apply this to what's happening to the two of you. You both have experienced an increased intimacy in your marriage. You're aware of the changes in your spouse's behavior which your spouse may or may not have noticed or, at least, isn't aware of yet. You're both beginning to take the time to exercise and relax. Betty, you've not only enhanced your self-image, but you've added some time with friends after work. You're both spending individual time with each other and with Ruthie. All these pleasures are variables which are conforming more to the way you want things to be. Thus, your *actions*, which are partially reflected in how you deal with others, are going to reflect the

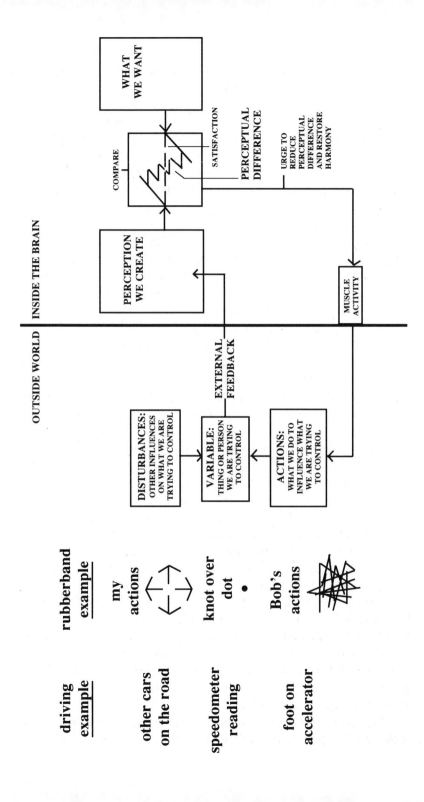

increased harmony within your system. You might not be aware of your external changes, since your mind is more centered on each other and the other areas of improvement, but those around you will surely notice. It's obvious to others that you have changed. All you have noticed is that what you perceive has become more the way you want things to be. Others see a change in your *actions*. As you said earlier, your friends at work noticed you as more relaxed. Remember, you had many **perceptual differences** that were contributing to your individual feelings of stress."

"What's a perceptual difference?"

"That's the difference between those things you wanted and how you perceived you were doing – your variables. Now that you've substantially reduced or eliminated many of these perceptual differences, there's been a marked improvement in how you feel. Obviously, your actions will reflect the increased harmony within your systems."

"But why have I lost weight?" she asked, looking puzzled.

"That's not unusual with those with whom I have worked. When people are in conflict, one of many ways of reducing the increased feeling of stress is by eating. Generally, high calorie food is perceived to be more pleasurable. Eating obviously doesn't solve the problem, but it does give a sense of relief from the stress that's felt. As you eliminate some of your conflicts, there's a reduction in tension or pain. Anytime there is a reduction in pain, it is perceived by our nervous systems as a good feeling. When you feel better, especially through the resolving of conflicts, there is less need to relieve stress through eating – so you eat less. Thus, you tend to return to more normal eating habits and lose excess weight. Many people gain weight by eating to reduce the pain of stress. Then, they lose weight by trying a diet or exercising. However, without a reduction in stress, they will more than likely return to eating as a way to ease the unresolved emotional pain.

"How about your list Bob? Has it been helping you?"

"To tell you the truth, I didn't really keep it too well the first week," he responded sheepishly. "It felt kind of strange and a bother. Also, I admit that I didn't think it would work. It sounded too simple. As I saw Betty's disposition begin to change, I realized there was really something to it, so I got back into keeping my list. I don't feel as concerned as I did before, but it's hard to think of good things that have happened. That should tell me something."

"Keeping my lists has certainly helped me, especially the one regarding the good things that Tim has been doing," Betty said.

"You're both catching on to these ideas quickly!"

"As I said, a lot of things have happened," Betty said excitedly. "June was home from school over the weekend, and it was obvious to her that things had really improved around the house. She began to ask questions, and I was explaining these ideas as best I could. Then I got the idea of asking her to give me her standards for the kind of man she wanted to marry. As you know, neither Bob nor I approve of her boyfriend. With this in mind, I told her how you helped us review our values, then set priorities, and then set our standards. I felt that if she would review her standards for the kind of husband she would like, she might see the disparity between her standards and her boyfriend. Obviously, I didn't say anything to her about my concerns.

"Well, she went right along with the idea, and she came up with a list. I did as you suggested – I got her to list what was important in the man she wanted as her husband. Then I had her set priorities in the list. Next, I asked her to match Charlie, her boyfriend, with her list to see how close he came to what she wanted. She started to compare, and I could see she was getting more and more uncomfortable with what she was discovering. Her boyfriend compared favorably with only five out of her fourteen standards, and only one of those was in the top five on the list. She didn't say anything about the list the rest of the weekend. As she kissed me good-bye, she whispered into my ear, 'I'm going to think about getting rid of Charlie. He's really not for me.' Then she smiled and left." Betty handed me a piece of paper. "She left the list, so I thought you might want to see it."

June's Husband Qualification List

1. sees me as equal *	8. spiritual – strong faith
2. not critical	9. expressive – cries & laughs
3. have a lot in common	10. successful career
4. has a warm family relationship	11. travel together *
5. unconflicted	12. sense of humor
6. good listener – pays attention *	13. likes children
7. honest *	14. attractive *

* qualifications that Charlie matches

Betty smiled and then, turning serious, said, "Ed, it must be a lot harder for single people, isn't it? I mean, Bob and I have had each other

all these years, and once our relationship began to improve, it really has
been helpful to have someone to talk to and depend on. I have several
employees at work who seem to be having problems, and I know they're
single. Knowing how helpful it is to work with Bob, I was wondering
how you help others who lack the same support system I have."

"I think everyone who comes to me for counseling has the need for
support in an area in which they're not too experienced. There is a good
chance that one or both of you wouldn't have kept your lists as faithfully
had I not kept checking on how you were doing. Many couples don't
stay with their quality time commitment unless I stay after them –
sometimes calling them up, making sure they're doing what they'd
committed themselves to doing."

"You call people up?" Bob said.

"Sure, Bob, if I think it is necessary. That's what this business is
all about. Had you or Betty slacked off in any way, I would have been
on the phone. I see that as part of my job.

"With regard to single people, Betty, you're right – especially
single parents. Those who live alone or without the support of another
committed adult need someone who acts as a support system – who
recognizes their accomplishments early on. They need someone who
encourages them, who cares, who gives a damn, and is willing to be
supportive of them over a period of time until they gain sufficient
confidence to be on their own. These are needs that I can satisfy.

"Eventually, as they start to build confidence on their own, they
begin to need me less and less. My job is to teach them how to build the
kind of self-image that will allow them to mature and grow. For many,
however, I remain a friend for life. They know I'm here. Some I see
once every six months to a year. They give me a call, and we talk over
how they're doing. I think that's what a counselor is – a teacher and a
friend and, for many, a surrogate parent. If you're all alone, without any
extended family nearby, there's nothing wrong with having someone
around on whom you can depend."

"You're right," Betty said. "I guess Bob and I are very fortunate."

"I'll second that," Bob added, smiling.

"At any rate, I'm happy both of you are doing so well. I know that
June has been one of your big concerns, Bob. Now, getting to what we
talked about two weeks ago, have either of you tried to deal in some way
with either a member of your family or with someone at work?"

"I did," Bob said. "I asked my boss for a meeting and tried to use
some of your methods. It went pretty well. He was upset at first and

very evasive. He even accused me of trying to pin him down – which I was! But I kept at him, and eventually he began to calm down, especially when I started writing down his answers." Bob laughed, then continued, "He demanded to know what I was doing, and I just told him I wanted to remember what he said so I wouldn't forget."

"That's a good technique, Bob. People tend to evaluate what they say when they see others writing down their thoughts."

"That part worked out pretty well, but the problem I'm wrestling with now is how do you deal with employees who do just enough to get by or are just on the edge of being arrogant or rude to others?"

"First, you have to make sure you have a solid, well-understood set of standards. Most standards are understood and accepted by people in the way they live their lives, but not set down in any rule book. For example, in most families, you don't just walk into a bathroom when it's occupied. As children are told to 'knock before you open' and as they become conscious of their own physical bodies, they tend to develop a sense of respect for another's privacy.

"Remember that standards aren't just for determining how we should act around others or to govern our choice of spouse, business partner, or employee. Standards are what make it possible for human beings to live at peace with each other and in harmony with themselves. State and federal legislatures create standards, as do city and county governments. Standards are around us everywhere, from traffic laws to smoking restrictions in public and private places.

"With children, I see standards and discipline as synonymous. I define **discipline** as *teaching people to obey standards and, eventually, to learn to set standards for themselves.* If we insist only that children obey the rules set by others but never help them to develop their own rules, they're going to function less efficiently as human beings. We set our values and priorities, but, to accomplish what we want in life, we need standards that reflect those values as practical criteria for our actions. Standards are the bridge between our value systems and the decisions we make every day.

"Telling people to drive safely without making sure they understand the rules of the road will bring chaos. The same will happen in a home. Some parents will announce a rule and then back down the minute the child tests it, or they will set no standards at all. Often their standards are out of line with the general community standards – cursing, taking and never returning a neighbor's tools, returning merchandise they've damaged and claiming it was sold in that condition.

The worst situation is when parents insist that their children follow standards that their behavior doesn't reflect. I remember one family which insisted that their children attend church every Sunday, but the parents stayed home. Many couples I've counseled had restricted their children's television time while they spent hours watching their favorite programs. I believe that's called hypocrisy.

"When you're dealing with others – whether at work or at home – you first have to establish standards that are clear, specific, understood, and reasonable. Then everyone, including yourself, must follow the same standards. Obviously, with growing children, standards will change as they mature and can handle more independence. When dealing with adults, you'll find that, without being told, most already have an understanding of what standards apply where. Here's a copy of the card I use when teaching responsibility through discipline.

"I have a former student and close friend, Susan Cooke, a high school librarian in Phoenix. She uses these counseling techniques in her library. To a student she finds reading with a filled plastic cup, she politely says, 'What's in the cup?' The reply might be, 'Soda.' Then she asks, 'What's the rule about bringing drinks into the library?' Invariably, the student looks down at the floor and says, 'You're not allowed soda in the library?' She then asks, 'Is what you're doing against the rules?' The student admits it is and commits to resolving the issue. Then she asks, 'What's your plan?' If the student decides to throw it out, she points the way to the sink. Or the student may decide to leave the library. Either way, she thanks the student.

"To students who are talking, she merely asks, 'What are you doing?' They usually say, 'We're talking.' Then she asks, 'What's the rule about talking?' They generally reply, 'You're not allowed to talk in the library.' Again, she gets an evaluation and commitment. Then she asks, 'What's your plan?' They either decide to leave the library to continue their conversation or remain and study. She's always polite and never raises her voice. She's never had to tell a student a rule.

"Once you have standards in place, the second thing you have to do is to find a hook – something that is sufficiently important to them that their present attitude is going to interfere with their achieving that goal. Take Tim as an example. Both of you have expressed concern about his general attitude around the house and his abusive language toward Betty. The role play we did last time was indicative of your problem with him. Betty, do you remember, in playing Tim, how I tried to work you toward establishing standards with which we could both live?"

TEACHING RESPONSIBLE THINKING
based on perceptual control theory - by Edward E. Ford

RESPONSIBILITY - The willingness and ability of people to follow standards and rules and ultimately to set their own, without infringing on the rights of others.

A. ESTABLISH STRONG RELATIONSHIPS

The most important step when teaching responsible thinking involves spending daily quality time alone with each person (see other side). People must believe you care about them and that you have confidence in their ability to resolve their problems. This allows you to access them more easily when there are differences.

B. SET STANDARDS; ASK FOR CHOICES & CONSEQUENCES

You need to **set specific and reasonable rules and standards** that must be **consistently applied** over time and **enforced fairly** with each person. When they are not willing to follow standards or obey rules, **ask them to name the various choices they have and to explain the consequences that result from making those choices.** The consequences should include the loss of the privilege which is related to the responsible choice they refuse to make.

Loss of privileges or restrictions must be the result of their not being willing to work at resolving their problem. Lifting restrictions or returning privileges should be tied to their having committed to a specific plan to resolve their problem. **Trying to control people by rewarding or punishing them doesn't teach responsible thinking.**

C. TEACH RESPONSIBLE THINKING

ASK THEM WHAT THEY THINK - KEEP QUESTIONING THEM - don't tell them what you think; ignore excuses & don't ask why; be non-judgmental; be specific & stay focused.

1. **Gather information:** Basic questions to ask are... *What are you (or were you) doing? What are the rules or standards? What are your choices and the consequences of those choices? What is it that you want now?*
2. **Compare:** Getting them to think responsibly... *Is what you're doing getting you what you want? Is what you're doing against the rules? Is what you're doing getting you all the things you want?*
3. **Commit:** Getting them to choose responsibility... *Are you willing to work at resolving your problems?*
4. **Teach them how to create a plan:**
   a. establish specific area of needed improvement
   b. set a measurable goal for needed feedback
   c. have them think through then explain in detail how they're going to achieve their measurable goal
   d. set up a chart which shows progress in time increments
   e. ask them if their plan is going to get them what they want and then ask them if they want to commit to the plan.

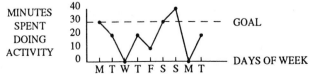

"Yes, I do," she replied. "I wanted to stay out later, and you eventually tied that goal to my grade point average. If I recall correctly, you tied getting my driver's permit, not only to my grades, but also to how well I got along with my parents and to earning enough money to pay for my part of the car insurance."

"The reason I did that was because, at least to my knowledge, no standards had been set regarding those areas. Tim was going about rudderless, so to speak. In response, you two were reacting rather than establishing agreements to some specific guidelines. In a very real sense, your systems concepts goal of happy, well-adjusted children had no well defined standards on which you could base your actions.

"I had to find what was more important to Tim than just going out and running around with his friends and being unpleasant and uncoop- erative around the house. He came up with wanting a driver's permit on his own. I found out that he did want to get along with the two of you, that he didn't enjoy the continual tension that he was experiencing. I also found out that he wanted to go to college and that was more important to him than his late night activities. Finally, he really wanted you to quit criticizing him, Bob. Betty, you must have picked these ideas up from things you've heard from Tim. Am I right?"

"I never really thought about them until we were doing the role play, but I know he's talked about going to college, and he has complained to me about how critical his father has been."

"Do you see how you try to find out what's important to the people with whom you work, so that you might help them deal more effectively with their problems?"

"Yes, I see that," Bob said. "I suppose it's the same thing you need to do to motivate people – finding out what's important to them."

"That's right, Bob. Managers, parents, and teachers are always looking for something external that will cause people to change. This assumes people are controlled by outside forces. A manager tries to encourage her employees to work harder by sweet talk, a pay raise, or the threat of losing their jobs. A parent wants his child to go to college, with little understanding of his child's goal to be a gunsmith or an electrician. People in authority want another person's goals to conform to their desires, which is trying to change another's control system. That's not how the mind works.

To motivate people, you have to find out what is important to them and discover if any of their goals align with what you want. Once both of you recognize a similarity in goals, then you have to work through a process of negotiations whereby you both come to an agreement, keeping the integrity of both of your control systems intact. That's exactly what I've been doing with you in these role plays.

"Sometimes, as a manager or parent, you deal with people who are struggling to build or rebuild a shattered self-image. Motivation here means trying to work at finding satisfaction through what is important to them while suffering a total lack of confidence in themselves. Often, people are concerned about your recognition of their importance to you, their sense of accomplishment or being in control, their being part of a team with input into the decision making process, or a combination of all three. **But, no matter whether their problem is establishing similar goals with you or the need to accomplish individual goals, you then have to teach them how to achieve what they want.** As they begin to realize control over gaining what they want, they will develop a certain awareness of creating their own satisfaction, that internal recognition that 'they're achieving something' and that others on their team, in their department or family acknowledge their importance and accomplishments. This ability to 'put things in their right order and control them well,' to quote Thomas Aquinas, whether through working cooperatively with another or through finding satisfaction in those areas within our systems concepts, our values and beliefs, is at the very heart of motivation. Your job is very important, though. You're their teacher.

"Now, Bob, do you have an employee that you want to role play with me that reflects the kind of person that you were asking me about?"

"I've got lots of them," he said, smiling. "Let me play Pete, one of my maintenance foremen. He's forever going around giving the people on the line a hard time. Whenever there is a breakdown and a repair is needed, he's responsible for getting things fixed. He's obviously not a happy person, and he's constantly harassing people – especially Beth, the line foreman I told you about. I've told him a thousand times to stay off her back, but he persists. He's very good at what he does, but sometimes when he fixes one mechanical breakdown, he leaves behind a human breakdown."

"O.K., Bob, let's try it. You're Pete, and I'll be you."

Bob (played by Ed):   "Pete, I asked you to come into my office because I'd like to chat with you for a few minutes. Do you have any idea what I'd like to talk about?"

Pete (played by Bob):   "Not a clue, Bob, what's on your mind?"

Bob (played by Ed):   "Let me ask you how you think you've been
                        doing?"
Pete (played by Bob):   "Well, I think I've been doing a good job. You
                        got any complaints?"
Bob: "When you say you're doing a good job, what do you think
            your job involves?"
Pete: "Primarily, it involves breakdowns on the production line."
Bob: "What else does it involve?"
Pete: "Well, if things are going well on the line, then I keep my men
            busy doing maintenance work around the plant and assisting
            the other crews."
Bob: "Is there anything else your job entails?"
Pete: "I have to make sure my men do their job."
Bob: "What does their job entail?"
Pete: "Doing the work they're assigned, not goofing off or playing
            around with any of the women on the line."
Bob: "What do you mean by 'playing around with the women?'"
Pete: "Talking to them when they should be working. I had trouble
            with one of them patting a few of the women on the ass. That
            kind of stuff can get this place slapped with a lawsuit."
Bob: "So you think that harassing women can get us in trouble?"
Pete: "Come on, Bob, you know it can."
Bob: "The women out there must appreciate the way you keep the
            men from hassling them. What do you think?"
Pete: "I don't know and, frankly, I don't care. Most of them are a
            pain to work with. Temperamental. Everything's personal."
Bob: "Pete, besides protecting the women from the harassment of
            your men, how do you think you're perceived by the women
            on the floor?"
Pete: "Oh, I don't know, I don't think that's important. If they
            don't like me, that's their problem. I do my job, that's what
            you pay me for."
Bob: "Do you think, being a foreman, that you represent the
            company when you're working on the floor, in the way you
            deal with the employees as well as your peers?"
Pete: "Look, Bob, I do my job, and that's what you pay me for."
Bob: "Do you represent the company when you're working on the
            floor, in the way you deal with others?"
Pete: "I don't know. I never thought about it. I suppose so, but
            what's the big deal?"

Bob: "So you believe you're perceived as the company to the employees?"

Pete: "Well yes, I guess so – at least part of the company."

Bob: "What's the company policy regarding how others should be treated?"

Pete: "I don't know, but I suppose everyone's to be treated the same, no favorites."

Bob: "Pete, do you think that you treat the people on the floor fairly and with no favorites, and with respect, the same as you demand from your men?"

Pete: "Well, I'm no worse than anyone else."

Bob: "You just told me a few minutes ago that you do your job, which is to keep the line running. I agree, you do a very good job of that. With regard to how people are treated, you just said you're no worse than anyone else. Does that mean there's an area in which you need to improve?"

Pete: "Well, I might be a little tough on people, but that's my nature."

Bob: "What do you mean 'tough on people'?"

Pete: "You know me, you know what I mean."

Bob: "I'm asking you, Pete, what you mean by being 'tough on people'?"

Pete: "I guess I'm a little abrasive, but that's my nature."

Bob: "If one of your men told you it was just his nature when he patted a female on the rear, how would you deal with that?"

Pete: "O.K., I get the message. I'll try to show a little more respect. Some of these people piss me off."

Bob: "Pete, do you think the way you treat the people on the floor, both your peers and the employees, needs improvement? Or are you satisfied with how you're doing?"

Pete: "Some of them can be so irritating."

Bob: "Are you satisfied with your performance in relation to how you treat people on the floor?"

Pete: "I guess I could stand to improve somewhat. Everybody needs improvement in that area."

Bob: "Do you need improvement in that area?"

   "Yes, I just said that I did."

Bob: "Is what you're doing now, the way you treat people, your abrasiveness as you described it – is this the area you want to improve?"

Pete (played by Bob):   "Well, yes. Obviously, you have a problem
                          with it, or you wouldn't have called me in here."
Bob (played by Ed):   "Do you really want to work at this?"
Pete: "Well, I can give it a try."
Bob: "Pete, do you want to work on this or not?"
Pete: "Yes, I do."
Bob: "All right, who was the last person you had difficulty with on
                          the floor – anyone – a foreman, one of your people, or one of
                          the people on the line?"
Pete: "You know what happened between me and Beth, I saw you
                          talking with her right after I got into it with her."
Bob: "What happened?"
Pete: "I had told her to keep an eye on a conveyor belt motor on
                          number two station where some of her people work, and she
                          didn't. The motor has a tendency to heat up and stop. I didn't
                          want to have to stop the line to replace the motor."
Bob: "So then what happened?"
Pete: "About an hour later, the motor overheated and stopped, and
                          I had to rush in and replace it."
Bob: "How did you deal with Beth?"
Pete: "I yelled at her because she didn't see the motor overheating
                          prior to the breakdown."
Bob: "What words did you say to her?"
Pete: "Well, I said something like 'dumb female' and called her a
                          few names."
Bob: "The way you treated Beth, does that meet the standards
                          you've set for your crew?"
Pete: "You know it doesn't."
Bob: "How would you have handled it differently?"
Pete: "Well, she should have known better."
Bob: "Had she been a man, would you have handled it differ-
                          ently?"
Pete: "O.K., so I was wrong."
Bob: "Supposing some equipment were to break down in her
                          station today, how would you handle it now?"
Pete: "I get your point. I'll go easier on her."
Bob: "Because she's a woman?"
Pete: "No, because things will work out better if I do."
Bob: "So, how are you going to handle it the next time something
                          breaks down?"

Pete: "O.K., I got your point. I'll treat her well, I promise."
Bob: "How can I be sure? You told me this the last time we
           talked?"
Pete: "Watch me, that's all I can say. This time I mean it."

"Gosh, you really keep a person focused, don't you?" Bob said. "I
tried to sidetrack you several times, and you wouldn't let me."

"In dealing with people, the kind of questions I ask gives me control
over the direction of the dialogue. People tend to allow this because I'm
showing interest and respect for their worlds, even though I'm getting
them to reveal their worlds and be responsible for them."

"I was fascinated by how you kept his feet to the fire. You really
didn't let him get away with anything," Betty said. "I'm surprised Bob
didn't get angry with you."

"I couldn't," Bob said. "I wanted to get angry and react, but I was
thinking of my responses to his questions. He wasn't saying anything
to me that was critical in any way. He just kept hammering relentlessly
at what I was doing, and getting me to make all kinds of evaluations and
comparisons. I kept feeling sort of defensive like I was being cornered
and there was nothing I could do. I couldn't admit my stupidity to my
boss, and yet he didn't make fun of me or in any way try to demean me.
His fairness in the way he treated me is what made it hard for me to get
angry with him. After all, he was using my words to deal with me, I
couldn't very well question the integrity of what he was saying. I just
felt trapped, but I also sensed I was being handled fairly and honestly."

"Well, if we have time, I would like to role play one of my personal
bankers, who has consistently come in late two or three times a week
for the past three or four months," Betty said. "I would love to be able
to handle him using your method."

"Fine, what are the rules about coming in late?"

"The handbook says that employees must come in on time, but the
consequences aren't spelled out. Hank is supposed to be at his desk at
eight thirty every morning. He recently got married, and he spends a lot
of time on the phone. I suspect he's talking with his bride."

"O.K., Betty. You're Hank and I'm you."

Betty (played by Ed):   "Hank, I called you into my office to find
           out how things are going. How long have you been with
           National Bank."
Hank (played by Betty):   "Four years next month."

Betty (played by Ed): "How do you think you've been doing since you've been here at this branch?"

Hank (played by Betty): "Oh, I think I've been doing pretty well. My sales are up on new accounts, and I don't think I have had any customer complaints about my performance."

Betty: "That's true, your sales are up, and there have been no customer complaints. Are there any other criteria by which you measure how you've been doing?"

Hank: "I get along with the employees here at the branch. I suppose that's important. And I work well with the various departments at corporate office."

Betty: "Fine, and are there any other criteria?"

Hank: "I guess I look presentable, you know, I dress O.K."

Betty: "Do you think you do well in the areas you've named so far?"

Hank: "Yes, I think I do."

Betty: "You're right, as far as I'm concerned. Is there any other area you can think of?"

Hank: There was a moment of silence. "Well, I put in my time. Sometimes I'm a little late, but I stay a little later to make up for it."

Betty: "Is there anything else you can think of?"

Hank: "No, I think that's about it."

Betty: "How about the proper use of phones, would you say that's a criteria?"

Hank: "Well, you know I've just gotten married, and Tracy and I are trying to buy a house and get some things done. Since she works nights, it's the only time we have to talk."

Betty: "Hank, what's the company policy concerning use of phones?"

Hank: "I guess I've been making too many personal calls."

Betty: "What's the company policy?"

Hank: "We're to use the phone only during lunch hour, and only if it doesn't interfere with the business of the bank."

Betty: "Is this what you've been doing?"

Hank: "No, I guess not."

Betty: "Is this something you want to work on?"

Hank: "Yes, it is. I'll just tell Tracy we'll have to work things out on the weekend or in the morning before I leave for the bank."

Betty: "You mentioned a few minutes ago you were a little late. What is the company policy about coming in late?"

Hank: "I'll be on time from now on. I mean it, I really will.

Betty: "Is there anything else you can think of in terms of how
           you're doing?"
Hank: "No, I guess we've covered everything I can think of. Did
           you want to see me for anything else?"
Betty: "No, that's all Hank. Thanks for coming in."

"It's just fascinating how you don't lecture, but rather get the
employee to deal with his own shortcomings," Betty said. "You even
let me tell you the company rules and regulations, and you weren't once
critical of me. I consciously tried to throw excuses at you, and you just
ignored them – just as you suggested we should a few minutes ago.
Even your tone of voice remains calm."

"You'll notice the difference between these two role plays. There
was really no defined company policy with the role play I did with Bob
playing Pete. Here I was having him really examine his own job
description, and, fortunately, he brought up the harassment of his
employees towards the women workers. I was then able to use that as
a vehicle to deal with his own sense of fairness about how he handled
others, especially Beth.

"The easy thing about talking with you, Betty, as you played Hank,
was that I had several well-defined company rules and I used them as
my wedge, and it worked well. The value of having very specific rules
can be seen in your role play of Hank."

"To tell you the truth," Betty said, "each branch is given the
autonomy to make its own rules. Having done the role play, I can see
how Hank would perceive that making up the time would be permis-
sible. But you handled that by bringing up the rule about being on time.
I felt trapped. When the misuse of the phone came up, I caved in quickly
so as not to have to deal with the embarrassment of not being on time.
I really learned a lot from doing that."

"Well, we're coming to the end of our session, and you two seem
to be doing pretty well."

"I want to come in again," Bob said. "I need a little more help in
working with some of my people. Especially if you have any ideas on
running efficient meetings."

"I agree," Betty said. "I'd like some help on teaching people how
to make and successfully complete their plans."

"Fine, I'll see you two weeks from today?" They both agreed.

Chapter 11

TEACHING PEOPLE
TO WORK TOGETHER

Several weeks later, I welcomed Bob and Betty to another session. "Nice to see you! How have things been going?"

"I haven't had a headache in three weeks, that's how things have been going," Bob said grinning. "I forgot to mention it two weeks ago when we were here, but it's just great! Also, about that list to help with the problem of my worrying, I found it strange at first. Now I find that, when I begin to worry, I catch myself and make a judgement about what I'm thinking. I often realize that it's something I can't do anything about, so I deal with those things that I can control. I just feel so much better. And, believe it or not, Betty and I haven't spoken a cross word to each other since we were last here. We still can't believe that things can change so much so fast."

"Betty, how about you?"

"It's true that Bob and I have really become a lot closer. And the younger children seem to be responding to your method, you know, asking them what they want and that sort of thing. It really does work, especially when Bob and I are getting along."

"Looks like you may not need me much longer," I said, smiling.

"No, not quite yet," Bob replied quickly. "But we're getting there, that's for sure."

"I tried your method on Hank, the personal banker with whom I've been having trouble," Betty said. "I had the questions written out in front of me on the desk to make sure I didn't make a mistake. Bob and I practiced the role play the night before so I'd be a little more confident when I faced Hank the next morning. And it worked. It really did! He hasn't been late since the interview, and the phone calls seem to have stopped. Your method does seem to get to the heart of a person's problems."

"Not always, Betty. Sometimes you work with a person and they seem to be doing well, then all of a sudden another problem surfaces." Betty gave a curious look and said, "What do you mean?"

"I've been working with a bright, articulate woman in her thirties who was divorced and has had several subsequent unsuccessful relationships. She worked for several months on improving a very low self-image and at building enjoyable relationships – especially within her family. She had been doing quite well until last week when she came in, complaining about feeling restless, not happy with herself. She had had several jobs, mostly with contractors, where she had always worked her way up to a lower management position but from which she had no further chance for promotion. She had finished high school and on and off had taken several unrelated courses at a local community college. When I asked her if she had ever thought of getting a college degree, she shrugged it off, as if it wasn't something she thought she could do. I challenged her evaluation of her perceived inability, pointing out to her all the work-related things she had accomplished over the years.

"The more we talked, the more excited she got. She had constructed very limiting goals for herself, which was probably due to her low self-image. Once she had built a better self-concept, the problem of her limiting job opportunities surfaced. Fortunately, she was just in time for the fall semester and is presently enrolled in two evening courses. She had resolved a number of problematic issues and began to feel good again. Then, all of a sudden, another unresolved issue suddenly surfaced – one she hadn't consciously thought through that was unrelated to the first problems and, apparently, of less importance. Once harmony is restored in one conflicting area, often other less important concerns begin to assert themselves.

"Bob, have you tried using these techniques with anyone?"

Bob smiled. "I sure did. I tried it with Pete, my maintenance foreman, who turned out much easier to work with than I thought he would be. He didn't bring up that his men harass some of the women on the line, but he admitted he had hassled Beth. I must say he has mellowed out quite a bit, but there are still a lot of rough edges."

"Is there anything else?"

"Oh, yes," Betty said. "We went to an Alanon meeting last week, and we've already learned some things we can do regarding how we can handle Mike. One thing for sure, we agreed not to lend him any more money until he has successfully completed an alcohol rehab program and is attending AA meetings regularly. They told us that the best way to tell whether people are really working at the program is by a change in attitude, increased enthusiasm in what they do during the day, and an increasing interest in others."

"You two are really moving ahead, that's for sure. I planned to cover two items today. One was how you get people to work more cooperatively with each other – whether it's at work or at home – through the use of meetings. The other was helping others to make specific plans, so they can manage whatever they are doing more effectively. Are you still interested in those issues?" They both nodded.

"Let's start with the use of meetings. I have done management consulting for a variety of companies. I've developed some ways of working with people – both individually and in groups – that make life easier for supervisors.

"There are two key questions. How do your people know what you want in terms of their own individual jobs, and, secondly, how do they know they're doing a good job? Control theory shows us that the more people understand what you expect from their job performance and the more often they get feedback on how they're actually meeting those goals, the more efficiently they work. This applies to any goal, whether self-imposed or imposed by a supervisor on the job – as long as the goals are specific and measurable. Once I set forty-five miles per hour as the speed I want to go – a specific, measurable goal – and I constantly glance at my speedometer – which is my feedback – then I will be able to keep my car at my desired goal.

"Control theory teaches that we control for input, which means that when I want something, I look for the results of my actions, the variable, and not the actions themselves. Actions are our output. In other words, I check the speedometer, not how hard I press my foot to the accelerator. Actions are not important except as a means to an end. The thing or person I'm controlling for is what I'm trying to change. I change my actions unconsciously, by changing my foot on the accelerator, to adjust to my own internal goal, which is to maintain a speed of forty-five miles an hour. This allows me to adjust the reading on the speedometer – my input – to conform to my goal – the precise speed I want to go. Are you both with me so far?" They both nodded.

"When you get a bunch of people, each with a unique control system, working together in the same location on the same project or toward the same general goals, then it is obvious you have to somehow align their worlds so that they can operate more efficiently. For people to work well together, what they must have in common are the same overall goals, even though their individual goals might vary according to each person's occupation.

"Another common thread should be that each person within the organization receives feedback that allows that employee to function efficiently as a control system. That means the feedback needs to have the kinds of measurements that reflect that employee's specific goals. Your goals probably include high quality, low costs, high volume, satisfied work force. Your maintenance foreman's goals are restricted to his area of responsibility, namely keeping the line operating with the least amount of downtime along with using his people efficiently when the line is running. Sales, marketing, quality control, production, manufacturing, engineering – they all have their own goals, tailored to their own area of responsibility. As the person that runs the factory, you have to make sure that all those various goals are aligned constantly, and, at the same time, each department must have the kind of feedback it can use to adjust to the constant changes inherent in the system. That is accomplished through meetings and simple measurement systems.

"I'd suggest a kind of meeting I learned about working with my friend, Harry, the plant manager I talked about before. I'd recommend a twenty-minute daily alignment meeting for each department first thing in the morning. Everyone at the meeting reports what their goals are for the day, what goals were accomplished the day before, and finally, where and from whom they need help.

"If these meetings have all been completed by eight thirty, then, about nine o'clock, schedule a regular manager's meeting about twenty minutes long with all your department heads. They tell you what specific goals are planned for that day, what goals were accomplished the previous day, and where and from whom they need help. All two-party problems are solved 'off line', outside the meeting.

"When there are any problems concerning the group that can't be resolved within the time constraints of the meeting, someone at the meeting is assigned the responsibility for taking action. That person has the A.R. – 'action required'. The person might form a sub-committee to resolve the issue. Ultimately, since the AR is by the person's name in the committee's minutes, there has to be a report back to the meeting on the final action on the problem. A summary of the goals and actions required from that meeting is sent to all department heads within an hour after the meeting.

"Finally, wherever the meetings are held, there should be one or more goal charts with measurements everyone can understand. The charts should reflect daily, weekly and overall goals that are measurable and reflect the decisions and actions of the people at the meeting. I remember once working with a foreman in the shipping dock of a carpet manufacturer. They were making two to three errors a week in carpet shipments, which were very costly. He put up a chart in his office, and each morning he met with his people and, among other things, reviewed the chart. He also asked for ideas for greater efficiency. Within a month, faulty shipments were down to two a month. People must have specific and daily feedback to work efficiently.

"This type of meeting does two things. First, you are continually aligning worlds at the various levels within your organization. Second, and probably more important, your people create a perception of themselves as part of a team and part of your company, not just as someone working for bosses.

"I've tried this with an executive housekeeper and her crew of cleaning personnel in a hotel chain. There was a reduction in the time it took to clean each room and an increase in the quality. I've even got a dentist friend doing this with his staff of three. They meet every morning, go over their individual plans, and he says the team work and office efficiency have increased dramatically.

"I've seen this happen in a large manufacturing plant, in small operations such as I just mentioned, and in a five-thousand-employee operation. If you understand control theory, you'll understand why and how this aligning of worlds works, and you'll be able to apply this within your own organization.

"People have to have goals and feedback if they are going to work efficiently. I remember asking a contractor how his foremen knew they were meeting the goals of each job on a daily or weekly basis. He said they didn't. I then asked him if his superintendent's knew, and he said he didn't think so. That same contractor filed for bankruptcy several months later. To me, one of the reasons was obvious."

"We do have a lot of meetings," Bob said, "but it never occurred to me to look at the meetings in terms of this control theory of yours. We don't have regular daily alignment meetings, as you call them, and I can see where a lot of problems would be eliminated if we did. I'm just getting used to thinking in terms of my own control system. I just never looked at people as control systems. Nor did I think of the need for aligning those systems so they would work more efficiently together."

"We do have staff meetings once a week at our branch," Betty said. "These are primarily to go over reports and to give anniversary or birthday recognition. I think your kind of meeting sounds different and is certainly held more often. I know managers go to too many meetings at the corporate office. I'll have to think how this could be applied to my branch. It does make sense. I like the idea that people can have the opportunity to ask for help, and that the employees will have a better understanding of what their peers do and the goals, problems, and accomplishments of the branch."

"How about at home? Do you think a family meeting might help?"

They both laughed. "I think there has been too much change already for the kids to handle," Betty said. "The reason we were laughing is that with June home over the weekend, we had a family meeting with the three youngest. We talked about goals and how we were getting along. It was hard not to be critical of what the children said, but we both held our tongues."

"Criticism will kill both a meeting and the support from the people attending the meeting," I said.

"What if someone says something stupid or just wrong," Bob asked. "How do you handle it?"

"It's amazing what happens when you ignore such remarks and say nothing. Just return the meeting to what you are focused on. When people say something that would distract the meeting, ignoring it means there is no payoff, and they are less likely to continue with distractions. When you ignore a remark, people are more likely to make a value judgement of what they said in terms of what they want. Reacting to what they say takes them off the responsibility hook."

"How about some ideas on helping people take responsibility for themselves, to be able to make plans," Betty said. "How does your control theory address this?"

"Once you understand that you are an internally-driven, closed-loop control system and are aware of what drives your system, applying these ideas to various aspects of human interaction becomes easier. As you recall, the first of the two things that control this system is what we want, which involves the various levels of control. Second, is our perceptual system, which is not only where we build our understanding of the world, but is also our feedback system.

"This feedback system is the input system of our brain. The feedback is what we are consciously trying to change. When you want to go forty-five miles per hour, what you are consciously trying to change is your speedometer. That's your input system. This simple idea is the hardest for people learning control theory to understand.

"Most people try to get you to change what they call your behavior or what I call your actions. They tell you if you would only stop yelling and screaming, making critical remarks, trying to control others – all of which we do without thinking – things would be better. But they are wrong! Why? *Because we think only about what we want and the input, which is our feedback, and not about our actions.* They want you to stop yelling because they don't want to deal with that input into their own systems. People aren't really that aware of what they're doing. It isn't obvious to them. They are concentrating on input, the results of what they are doing, not their actions, their output. That is why giving lectures to people about *what not to do* is so futile, unless they perceive you as a teacher and want to learn from you.

"As both of you have found out, you began to fall in love again when your perceptions of each other started to improve. You were already committed to working at the relationship. Once your wants and perceptions became aligned, your actions – or behavior, if you wish – began to change automatically to reflect that new alignment.

"As you began to perceive Betty as more loving and enjoyable to be with, Bob, this input or feedback into your system began to conform to what you wanted, a more loving and caring Betty. Your actions just conformed to this new alignment, just as you no longer increase the pressure on the accelerator when you've reached your designated speed. Understanding this concept allows you to design a way to help others improve their performance, whether it's in the home or at work.

"Along with my good friend, Jim Soldani, a business consultant, I designed a performance appraisal that conforms to the concepts of control theory. This could be used by parents trying to help their children improve as well as by managers with their employees. All employees should do their own appraisals. It should always be written out completely by the person whose performance is being reviewed. The person then presents it to the designated supervisor and a short conference is held regarding the employee's performance.

"The appraisal form has two sections. The first asks people to list one specific area in which they do their job well. The second asks them to list one area where they believe they need to improve.

"In the first section, they have to list two examples that substantiate their claim, along with detailed accounts reflecting all the particulars of what happened. What this does is keep them from making claims that can't be substantiated. It keeps the report honest.

"Asking them to list an area where they need to improve is a little more complicated. First, the employees should list an area of performance they believe needs improving. This could be the way they deal with others – an appropriate area for Pete, Bob's maintenance foreman. Or it could be coming late to work – where Hank, Betty's personal banker, needed to improve. The key is that the employees choose the area for improvement, not the manager. After the first two or three evaluations, the manager should feel free to suggest an area."

"What if employees continues to skirt around some problems they've been having?" Bob asked.

"If you as a manager should find employees ignoring an important area of needed improvement, then you should bring it up as a suggested area they consider. If any of them keep trying to avoid the issue, then you ask those people to include the area in question in their next appraisal evaluation.

"Now, once they have listed the area for improvement, then next they have to write down a way they plan to measure this improvement. They should include at least one goal chart."

"Aha!" Betty said, smiling. "This is the necessary feedback our system needs so we can operate more efficiently, the input you were talking about."

"That's right. This is a critical part of plan making. If I say I'm going to do something, I should be able to measure the results. The more specific the measurements and the more the feedback reflects those measurements, the more likely I am to accomplish my goals. A goal chart that measures daily, detailed accomplishments, hourly if appropriate, is necessary if the person's performance is to improve.

"I was once teaching these ideas in an eight-week marriage course and several weeks after I mentioned this feedback concept, a woman raised her hand and announced she had lost seven pounds. Since it wasn't a weight reduction course, I was somewhat taken aback until she explained. She said she had written down everything she had allowed herself to eat and when to eat it. Then, as feedback, she wrote down everything she did eat and the time. She said writing things down at the moment of action forced her to make a value judgement. She said she had been tempted to quit making the list, but with this method, she knew that either she'd stop keeping the list or she'd lose weight."

"I suppose we can use this same idea with Tim and Ruthie," Bob said. "It might work both for their homework and their chores around the house."

"Absolutely. Remember, they have to be committed to the goal. Once the goals have been defined, then the next step is making the plan itself. This is where you become a teacher – either as a manager or parent – based on your own experience in the area in which you're helping the person. If you're going to work with someone, you should have at least some competence in the area where you're helping. If all my children were having severe problems dealing with their lives, I don't think I'd be very qualified to help others deal with their offspring.

"There are many elements to good plan making. I personally like my clients to **take notes when making a plan**, it keeps the perceptions aligned. Also, it's critical that, when you make a plan, you **stay focused on the plan** and not wander off, talking about other things. It's important that **the plan should be something a person really can do**. Otherwise, you're setting the person up for failure. Self-confidence comes from attaining goals, not failure.

"I can see that easily enough," Betty said. "You focused us on how we could eliminate our conflicts, including a very unhappy marriage, by having us concentrate on what we could do. That's no doubt why our lives have gotten so much better so quickly. We didn't deal with the unpleasant past, how upset either of us was, or what we didn't like about the other person. You realized that would only have made the problem worse.

"I think anytime a person makes a plan, **it should begin at once**," I continued. "The old saying 'Strike while the iron is hot' is all too true. Also, the sooner improvement is experienced, the more likely the plan will succeed.

"Now, remember, **never allow people to make plans that are beyond their abilities to succeed at the time**," I cautioned. "Because we believe the plan is feasible and easily accomplished doesn't mean that it would be for the person with whom you're working. I doubt if Pete would have been able to turn his disposition around as quickly as you might have thought. After all, he's designed that style of dealing with others and has used it for many years. People don't redesign their systems that quickly.

"The greatest help you can give others who are attempting to improve their lives is yourself. **Show a committed interest in what they are doing.** I recently saw a young woman in her thirties whose self-image was so low, it was hard for her to do the simplest tasks with any consistency. She had made a plan to take a twenty minute walk every day. I involved myself in her plan by having her call me daily after she had fulfilled her plan. She did that for two weeks. That was two months ago. Today she no longer needs to call and enjoys daily walks.

"Quite often, I'll call couples within a few days after I've seen them to make sure they are working at their plan. This is my involvement in making sure they're not goofing around. It also shows I care, which is a major source in helping people develop a belief in themselves. After all, self-confidence and a healthy self-image begin with someone who believes in you. How else can you develop a strong self-image, except through another who takes the time to care? That feedback is what you use to construct your self-image. That's the most important part of helping others."

"I must admit I was surprised when you called me several days after I'd seen you," Bob said. "I've never had that happen before. I don't know, it just gave me the feeling that you were really interested. That's a rare quality today."

"The critical thing is to **make sure people are involved and committed to making a plan.** When they bring in a plan already thought out, then there is no reason to believe they aren't committed. When dealing with any of your children – as I did in your role play of Tim, Betty – you have to make sure they not only have made the proper value judgements concerning the inconsistencies in their world, but that there is a strong, positive commitment to making a plan. Without a strong commitment, you're not likely to see many plans accomplished.

"Once a plan is made, **there has to be an acceptance of what has been worked out**. There may well be revisions as you work out the details during your meeting. One way to make certain that people accept the final plan as belonging to them is to get both a positive evaluation as to the acceptability of the final plan and a firm commitment to its fulfillment. Otherwise it's highly unlikely the plan will succeed. The stronger the internal signal that reflects a commitment to the plan, the more likely will be its completion.

"At the end of a plan-making session, **always make certain that the person for whom the plan is being made summarizes exactly what the improvement is, what the goal is, along with the specifics of the chart, and the details of the plan.** Everyone involved needs to agree on what is going to happen as a result of the plan. What you're doing here is aligning the world of the manager or parent with that of the person with whom you're working. Again, an understanding of control theory demands a continual alignment of the various worlds involved if harmony between the systems is going to be maintained.

"Finally, **there should always be a date set for the next meeting**. The kind of performance appraisals I'm talking about for the workplace could take place every six to eight weeks, but I'd never go more than two months without such a reappraisal. Then, when it comes to determining promotion or a salary increase, all you do is pull out your employee's own record of performance and you've got something that is tangible and easily compared to company standards. In the case of a promotion, the file is easily reviewed by someone who has never met the person being considered. That factors out the opinion of a supervisor who could be biased in either direction."

"And I can see this working well in helping us deal with the children," Betty said. "It allows them some say as to what they're going to do. It teaches them to make plans."

"Isn't that the essence of what this is all about – helping people take responsibility for their own lives?"

"Yeah, I guess it is," Betty said.

"Well, I guess our time is about up. Do you want to come back?"

"We seem to be doing pretty well, and we can always call if we need you," Bob said. "How about you, Betty. Do you want to come back?"

"No, I think things are going along pretty well," she responded. "As Bob said, we can call if we want to make another appointment. I do appreciate all that you've done for us."

"I'd like to leave you both with a thought," I cautioned. "Most people, when their lives begin to improve, tend to quit doing what was helping them. It's as if they hadn't quite made the connection between their improved state in life and what they have done to bring that about."

"I can see that happening to us," Betty said, seriously. Bob frowned and nodded.

"I'd suggest that you take a yearly calendar and mark off the last Sunday in the month for the whole year, to remind yourselves to review what you have been doing for the month just past. You're both in business. It could be seen as a regular monthly review of operations, only this time it would be concerning your life."

"I like that idea, Ed," Bob said. Betty nodded.

"Thanks again, Ed," Betty said, smiling. "You did a lot for us."

"Betty, you did the doing. I did the teaching. Oh, yes, I have one last card for you – Freedom from Stress."

"We can't thank you enough," Bob said. "Thanks for everything."

As Betty gave me a hug on the way out the door, she whispered, "I threw out the diaries."

FREEDOM FROM STRESS
based on control theory
Edward E. Ford, M.S.W.

The feelings you identify as stress can result from: two incompatible goals, a goal over which you have no control, emotional problems, and self-criticism.

To reduce stress, examine what you really want:

First — **list those things in your life that are important to you, your values and beliefs**, those things that make up your blueprint for a satisfying life. These may include spouse, children, job, sports, parents, friends, health, or faith.

Second — **prioritize** the above list in order of what is important to you. Is your spouse first, your faith second? Or, is your job first? What's third and fourth? Then, **evaluate** whether your values and the way you have prioritized them are giving you the satisfaction you want.

Third — **set standards or guidelines** that are based on your prioritized list. These standards will be your guide for the decisions you make when trying to achieve what you want.

Fourth — **list the specific, measurable things you could do** to accomplish what you want based on your standards.

Deal with specific areas of conflict:

Two incompatible goals of perceived equal importance — Evaluate how you have prioritized your values and decide which is more important.

A goal over which you have little or no control — Decide which specific values the goal represents, then choose another pathway to satisfy those values.

Emotional problems such as anger, depression, anxiety, and guilt — All feelings represent energy produced by what you want. Ask yourself "What do I want that I'm not getting that is causing me to feel the way I do?" Then deal with what you want.

Self-criticism that limits our ability to develop a satisfying life — Write down each day two things you do that are good and never repeat anything already on the list.

Epilogue

I called Bob and Betty several days later to make sure they had written their monthly reviews of how they were doing on their calendar. They had forgotten, but promised to do it.

Eight months later, I was invited to their twenty-fifth wedding anniversary celebration. Bob took me around, introduced me to his friends as the guy who taught him how to be happily married. Mike, their oldest, continues to drink, but Bob and Betty still attend Alanon meetings and have learned to deal with him and his problem. June broke off with Charlie and has no serious boyfriend right now. She's due to graduate from the university and has accepted a position with a bank in Tucson. Tim has settled down, but still has yet to get his driver's license. When his grades are up to the agreed standards, he hasn't the insurance money. When the money is available, his grades drop off. He and Bob play golf at least once a week. Ruthie continues to be a little charmer and gets her separate quality time with each of her parents every evening.

Bob's boss mellowed somewhat and then left the company for another job. Bob gets along well with the new vice president and, needless to say, is a lot happier at work. Betty has lost weight and her former relationship is a thing of the past. She's also been named an assistant vice president of her bank and continues as branch manager.

Me? I'm still teaching people control theory as a way to solve their own problems and writing an occasional book.

A PERSONAL AFTERWORD

"Nothing that enters from outside can defile that person; but the things that come out from within are what defile." Mark 7:15

We are a self-directing species, with our own internal control systems that are responsible for 'the things that come out from within.' In control theory, the beliefs and values that emanate from our systems concepts reflect our own self-designated blueprints for life – the way we believe our lives ought to be. How we construct our beliefs and values and the resulting happiness is largely based on the reliability of our blueprint and how honestly we adhere to the standards we've set and the decisions we've made.

As I reflect back over the hundreds of people I have seen, I note that very few have included a faith in what recovering alcoholics call *a higher power* when they reveal those things that are important to them. The solid Judeo-Christian values that permeated my childhood environment seem to have disappeared.

As I listened to Mark's words being read in church recently, I began to wonder how far many of us have drifted from the God-centered life we once knew. I wonder, if we were to use the values of our youth as an inspiration for our blueprints, perhaps our decisions would be more certain, more wisely directed, and lead us to a more satisfying and fulfilling life. Then I am reminded of St. Augustine's famous lament, "Our hearts are restless until they rest in Thee, O Lord."

APPENDICES

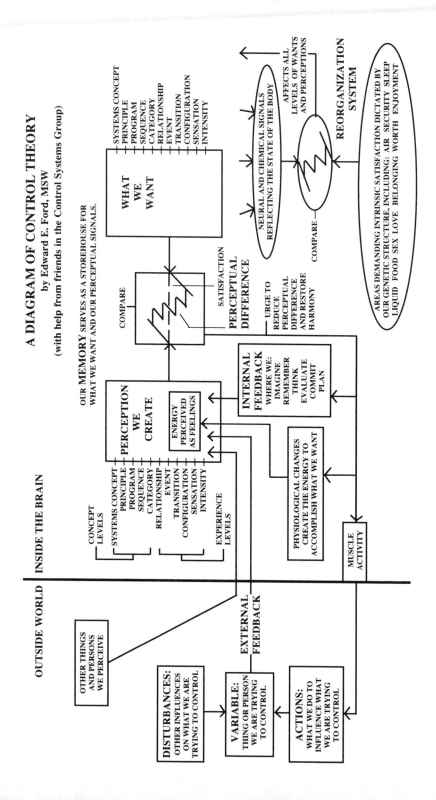

A DIAGRAM OF CONTROL THEORY
by Edward E. Ford, MSW
(with help from friends in the Control Systems Group)

Appendix 2

APPLYING PERCEPTUAL CONTROL THEORY TO EDUCATION AND PARENTING

Introduction

Since publishing the first edition of this book in 1989, I have developed a training program for school teachers, administrators, counselors, and especially parents, showing how to teach *responsible thinking* to children.

It began when I received an order for 50 copies of the first edition of *Freedom from Stress* from Frank Alessi at the Johnson City Central School District, Johnson City, New York. I phoned Frank regarding his interest in my book, and that began a long and close friendship with one of the most sincere and dedicated educators I've ever met. Frank introduced me to John Champlin, former superintendent of Johnson City Schools, who, during his 10-year tenure, had developed a powerful program for improving the educational level of children. Frank, a school administrator, is Project Director of the program John developed. Most school improvement efforts fail due to piecemeal, fragmented efforts; John's program is a comprehensive and systematic program to ensure conditions in which all students can learn with excellence, all teachers can teach more effectively, and all administrators can manage more competently.

Four key ideas guide his program. First is the belief that "we can be better." Renewal becomes a way of life and work. A viable and renewing organization needs individuals who are constantly growing and redefining excellence at higher levels of quality. Second, every facet of an organization's operation must be open to examination and change. There can be no exempted or shielded areas. Third, an organization must change in accordance with the best available research. The individuals in an organization must delve into this research, select that which is most important, and translate it into effective practice. Fourth, those in an organization must keep their focus on clear and compelling goals or outcomes. Everything that each individual in an organization does must align with and support these outcomes.

Living in accordance with these ideas has enabled school districts to improve student achievement and to produce conditions enabling teachers and administrators to be highly effective. For well over a decade, this program has been diffused to dozens of schools across the nation. Many of these adopters have achieved such high levels of excellence that they have been able to train still other districts.

John asked me to develop a parenting program for school districts. He felt that the only missing part of his program was that it didn't bring parents into the school district's process of rethinking and reorganizing. Thus was born my Teacher-Parent Program. The following is a summary of the program, showing, in particular, several worksheet forms developed while working with school district personnel and parents throughout the country.

I wish to dedicate this portion of my book to my two friends, Frank Alessi and John Champlin. I have worked with Frank in presenting training programs, and we have spent hours on the phone, rehashing and improving our approaches and ideas. His integrity and dedication to his work are inspirations to anyone who has worked with him or who has been taught by him. John Champlin's confidence in what I could do and his continued encouragement and support are much appreciated, especially coming from such a nationally recognized educator. I've never met anyone so dedicated to revolutionizing the educational system by teaching school districts methods of overhauling and improving the ways we educate our children. His dedication to American youth and his belief that all children can succeed drive him continually to wake up school districts throughout the U.S. It has been my good fortune to count both of these men as close friends.

Understanding Perceptual Control Theory

Every sound program needs an equally sound theoretical basis. Perceptual Control Theory (PCT) is based on a model developed by William T. Powers and researched by members of the Control Systems Group. In this book, I have attempted to present PCT and to show how it can be used *practically*. Below is a briefer presentation which I have found to ease the process of introducing the basic ideas of Perceptual Control Theory to parents and teachers.

Hunter wasn't Mrs. Johnson's favorite fourth grade student. He had been in trouble for most of the week, getting out of his seat and wandering around the classroom, talking when she was trying to teach the class, and constantly borrowing pencils and paper.

Today, Hunter was supposed to be working on his spelling. He didn't want to do his spelling — he wanted some attention. Sally Ann, who was busy doing her work, sat across the aisle from Hunter. He thought she was cute, and he liked her happy smile. He wanted her to notice him.

"Sally Ann, psst! Hi!" She looked over, smiled and giggled, then looked down at her paper. For a short time, Hunter had gotten what he wanted. He perceived Sally Ann's smile and giggle as signs of affection and caring. He wanted the pleasure to continue. Again, he tried to get Sally Ann's attention. "Psst, Sally Ann, hi!"

This second attempt at getting Sally Ann's attention did not go unnoticed by Mrs. Johnson. She looked at Hunter and asked, "Hunter, what are you doing?" Hunter looked up and said nothing. Then he pretended to return to his spelling exercise, while writing a note to Sally Ann.

What did Hunter want? He wanted some attention, and specifically, he wanted Sally Ann's attention. And what did Hunter see, or *perceive*? He perceived Sally Ann as working at her desk, ignoring him, not caring about him. Hunter compared what he wanted with his perception and found that there was a big *difference* between his goal and his perception. That difference caused him a lot of pain.

Now, how do you suppose Hunter tried to get rid of the pain which was caused by the difference between wanting Sally Ann to notice him and what he saw, which was Sally Ann busily doing her school work? Obviously, he tried to get her attention by making noise and calling her name.

What do you think was *most* on Mrs. Johnson's mind? What was she thinking about at the time Hunter called to Sally Ann? Think about your own life and how you handle things. Suppose one of your own children is yelling at another child; what are the dominant concerns in your mind? They probably are that you want to maintain quiet in the house and that you don't want your children fighting.

Imagine being Hunter's teacher, trying to maintain quiet in her class, making sure her students were busy so she could correct papers while Hunter was trying to get a little girl's attention. What is the first thing that would come to your mind? Obviously, you would want Hunter to do his work and not disturb other children.

The point is that *what comes to our minds is what we want.* The reason it comes to our minds is that something occurs in our environment which does not compare favorably to something we want. In the case of a parent, it could be yelling and screaming replacing the calm in the house. To a teacher, it could be talking in the classroom. If I were walking down the street with my wife, Hester, and a car were to drive by at what I consider to be a reasonable speed, I'd probably not give the car's passing a second thought. But if it were to drive by at 80 MPH, that would conflict with my own internal goal of what a safe speed should be.

Nothing around us ever bothers us unless it fails to conform to our own internally set goals or desires. It is comparing what is happening around us to what we want that drives us to *act*, but *only* when there are differences between the two. If everything compares favorably, then we don't have any concerns, and we don't act. Thus, in Hunter's case, what drove his actions is the difference between his goal and what he saw in his environment.

Human beings act when they are trying to change the outside world to make it conform to internally set goals. In Hunter's case, he acted by making the noise "Psst."

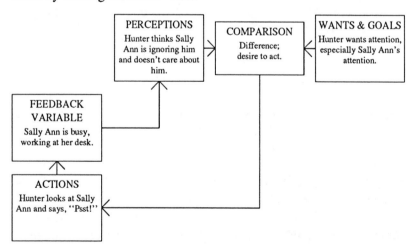

And it *worked*, because Sally Ann looked at Hunter, smiled, and giggled.

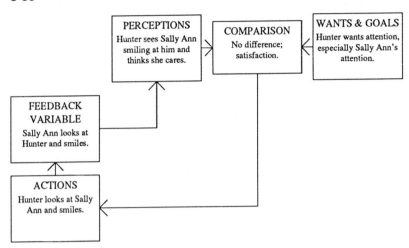

But it worked only *temporarily*. Sally Ann soon stopped paying attention to Hunter, and again there was a difference between his goal and his perception. So Hunter again acted to try to change the outside world to conform to his goal. This time, however, something else happened. Mrs. Johnson, the teacher, disapproved of Hunter's actions. She asked Hunter, "What are you doing, Hunter?" Hunter said nothing and pretended to go back to work. In Hunter's world, Mrs. Johnson was a *disturbance* affecting his ability to act in such a way as to perceive what he wanted.

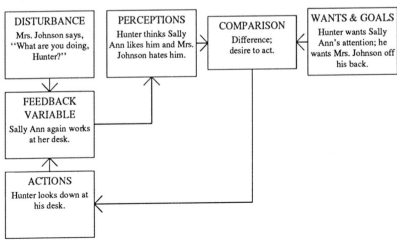

Hunter was afraid to continue saying "Psst!" to try to get Sally
Ann's attention. He now had to look busy to get around Mrs. Johnson's concern for noise. But there was still a difference between his
desire for Sally Ann's attention and his perception of Sally Ann. So
he tried an *alternative* action in an attempt to *get around* the disturbance (Mrs. Johnson) and to achieve his primary goal of getting
Sally Ann's attention. Hunter sent Sally Ann a note.

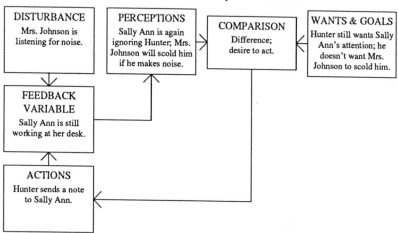

Guess what — it worked! Sally Ann looked at Hunter, smiled
again, and Hunter was again satisfied. This movement produced no
noise, and Mrs. Johnson, who wanted quiet in her room, was satisfied
that the noise had stopped. And it had. Hunter had evaded the disturbance and had gotten what he wanted.

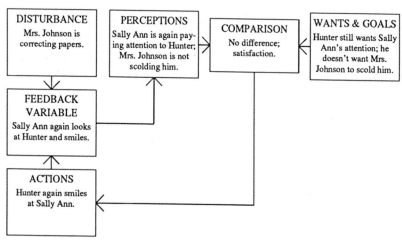

The above illustrates the basic ideas of Perceptual Control Theory. In short, PCT says that what drives us to do what we do is our comparing what we want to how we see things, and if there is a difference between them, we act to correct that difference, either by changing what we want or by acting to change what doesn't conform to what we want. *The details of how we perform the actions are of little importance to us. Getting the environment to conform to what we want is our major concern.* We act in *whatever* ways are necessary to perceive what we want to perceive, and we attempt to get around any disturbances we encounter. For those who are interested, there is much more about Perceptual Control Theory in the references given in Appendix 3 of this book.

Making Practical Use of Perceptual Control Theory

The most important key to rearing children is how you spend time with them. We all create our own perceptions and ideas of the world we live in, including our concepts of those with whom we live. Your children create their perceptions of you from those of their experiences in which you are involved, and also from those in which you are not. From my experience in working and consulting in schools, corrections, mental health, and residential treatment centers over many years, plus raising my own eight children, I believe that nothing is more important than our individual alone time with each of our children. Children create their perceptions of you based on the time you have spent with them and the *quality* of that time. We tend to listen to and respect those whom we perceive respect us, who care about us, and have expressed, both verbally and by their actions, a belief that we have worth as a human being.

What gives a teacher or a parent access to working with children is when the youngsters believe that whoever is working with them cares about them and believes in their ability to resolve their problems. Thus, the most important step when teaching responsible thinking involves spending the kind of time which is going to create this belief on the part of children that someone cares about them. I call this quality time, as discussed in this book and in more detail in my book *Love Guaranteed.*

This belief creates a willingness of children not only to resolve problems, but also to do so *cooperatively with those who spend individual alone time with them.* Over the past 30 years, I have taught

couples and parents with children how to build sufficient strength in
their marriages and families so that they could resolve their problems
in reasonable and rational ways. Quality time is the only effective
program I've found that will create the kind of love and trust that is
needed for relationships to survive and grow.

From Perceptual Control Theory, I have learned that we create
our perception of others from mutual, interactive types of experiences people have with each other. The criteria for these experiences
are as follows: first, whatever you do, you must be *aware* of each
other; second, you must *create* the enjoyment, rather than passively
watch TV or a movie; third, you must spend this time *alone together*
with whomever you are trying to build a relationship; and fourth, this
activity should happen on a *daily or regular basis*.

The second key to raising children has to do with creating an atmosphere in which they have a chance to develop responsibility. Responsibility is the willingness and the ability to obey rules and standards, and ultimately to set one's own, without infringing on the
rights of others to do the same. This means that the parent must set
standards and rules which reflect the parent's own values and beliefs,
and that the parent must then follow through with the natural consequences of not following the rules. All children eventually must
learn to respect the rules of the culture in which they live, or they
will be in conflict with people in that culture. My experience with
my own children has taught me that children tend to adopt the standards and values of their parents *if* they've established a close, loving
relationship with them, and *if* the choices they have made that reflect
the values and standards in the home have brought them a satisfying
life.

Ultimately, if children perceive you as caring about them, as
believing in them, and if they recognize the existence of reasonable
standards within the home, they are more likely to work cooperatively to find a way to get along.

Because no one can control another person's control system, I
begin my school district training programs by teaching the participants to just ask questions. Assuming that children are willing to
talk with you, the only way you can access them is through asking
questions (that's the reason for establishing strong relationships).
You explore. It is only through questions that they will examine
their own world. You find out what they want, how they perceive
various things, and what actions they are taking to achieve their

goals. Then you ask them what choices they have and what are the consequences for making each choice. (See Chapters 9 and 10 in this book.) This is the first step toward taking responsibility.

Next you ask them to compare their goals with their perceptions. They make a comparison, and in the act of making that comparison, they evaluate whether their actions are working and whether their actions are against the rules. They might also evaluate whether they are willing to live with the rules, change them, or whatever. Finally, you ask them if what they're doing will get them *all* of the things they want. For example, they might be getting *one* thing they want when they take a ball from another child, but they won't get *other* things they want, such as spending recess in the playground and enjoying time playing with their friends, if they continue their irresponsible thinking and consequent actions.

If they recognize and are willing to admit that what they are doing is against the rules and/or isn't getting them what they want, then you can go on to the next step, asking for a commitment. This step tests the strength of a want, such as the willingness to work at getting along with you. "Do you want to work at resolving the problem?"

Then, teach them how to make a plan. Once you ask them to establish a specific area of needed improvement, you ask them to set a *measurable* goal. They cannot attain a goal unless they establish a *specific* want and *specific* feedback that reflects that want. Imagine driving down the street and observing a traffic sign that says, "Drive at a Safe Speed." What speed would you drive? And even if the sign said, "Speed Limit 55," if your speedometer wasn't working or just wiggled up and down, then you still couldn't achieve the goal of driving 55 MPH. Most children are never taught to make effective plans, because teachers have no idea how the brain works. There is a need for both a specific goal and feedback that correlates exactly with what we want. Thus, the necessity for a feedback chart that reflects exactly what we are doing so that we can know how we are doing.

The diagram on the next page is a feedback chart, reflecting Perceptual Control Theory. The goal represents what we want. As we mark down how much time we spend on our activity, what we begin to see is the historical representation of how we've been doing. When you look at this chart, you are literally comparing your goal with how you've been doing, exactly the way the brain operates.

The differences between your goal and how you've been doing are what drive you to improve.

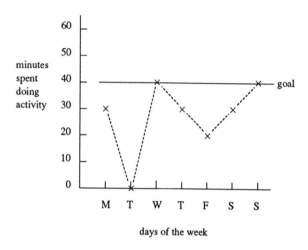

days of the week

If, while writing this, I felt thirsty and wanted a glass of water, I would do a number of things, including getting up from my desk, getting a glass from the kitchen shelf, turning on the faucet, filling the glass, and lifting the filled glass to my lips. The result of all of these various actions, each done without much thought, would be the perception of my thirst being quenched, matching what I wanted. In this example, I never think much about what "my actions" are, because my attention is centered on getting relief from my feeling of thirst. While most people try to change what others are doing, PCT suggests dealing with what they're *thinking*, namely their various wants, and how they perceive their present situation in relation to those wants. The important point here is that while most teachers, school counselors, and parents attempt to deal with the actions of their students or children, the key to helping these children is to teach them to deal effectively with what *causes* those actions, namely, how their children think.

There are two forms which use the feedback chart in my Teacher-Parent Program. The first form is titled "Performance Plan for Quality Time" (Form One, shown on page 191), which should be used by parents to keep track of how well they are spending time with their children. The second form is titled "Performance Plan for Improvement" (Form Two, shown on page 192). This can be used by parents and teachers when working with children who need help improving their performance.

Making Responsibility Possible

Whether people live or work together or both, they have to learn to get along. This involves cooperatively establishing standards and rules upon which they can base their actions. Standards allow people to go about satisfying their individual goals, sometimes involving direct interaction with other members of the community. Agreed-to rules allow everyone to make decisions in ways in which they don't infringe on the rights of others.

Living with others in accordance with standards and rules is something that all children must learn if they are going to be able to function effectively wherever they live. In family life, in the workplace, on the highway, in a restaurant or theater, there are always rules and standards, and, whether we like it or not, there are always consequences that flow from not following those rules or standards. If I were to walk into a home and mark up a wall with my pen, pick up a dish and throw it onto the floor, or set fire to a new sofa, there would certainly be consequences. In the community at large, if I drove 55 MPH through a school zone, took merchandise from a store without paying for it, or indiscriminately shoved people off a sidewalk, there would certainly be consequences.

The determination and administration of the consequences that result when a person does not follow certain rules or standards often have little to do with the choices made by the offending person. In some cases, the consequences are administered as deterrents to the person's actions and will vary in kind depending on who is in charge. In all cases, consequences are events, good or bad, that occur when children break the rules, whether at home or at school.

Perceptual Control Theory shows us that people react to consequences, sometimes called punishments or rewards, based on what they want and how they perceive the situation, *not* on what others do to them, and, as such, punishment and rewards are not an effective way to control children. This theory also shows us that for each of us to be able to achieve our own goals in life while interacting with others, we must adhere to the agreed-to rules and standards that allow us to make our own individual choices while respecting the rights of others.

To succeed, when children go to school, they have to learn to obey rules while, at the same time, respecting the rights of others, so that they can learn to function not only in the school, but at home, when they get a job, and when they get married and start their own families. If children are taught to deal with life in a way that allows the fewest hassles and the most satisfaction, then they must learn to respect rules and standards for the reasons they are promulgated, namely as guides to making the best choices while living with others.

I've already discussed discipline in the body of this book (page 147). The important key to discipline, whether at school or at home, is that if children persist in breaking the rules, they're given a choice as to whether or not they want to be removed from wherever they are to a more restricted area. Once in the restricted area, be it their bedroom, a school time-out room, a happy chair, or a quiet corner, it still must be their choice as to when they are ready to leave wherever they are and return. The requirement for returning to wherever they were is that they must be willing to work on a plan to deal with others when similar problems arise in the future. *Parents and teachers don't make these choices, the children do.* That is how responsible thinking is taught. They are given the choice and from this they learn that whatever happens to them is in their hands. That's what learning responsibility is all about.

Thus, in order for parents to deal with a child, they have to set specific and reasonable rules and standards that must be consistently applied over time and enforced fairly with each person. On those occasions when children are disruptive and hurtful of others, the parents will then have some already established standards with which to help them deal with these children.

When children are not willing to follow standards or obey rules, they should be asked to name the various choices they have and to explain the consequences that result from making those choices. The consequences should include the loss of the privilege which is related to the responsible choice they refuse to make.

Loss of privileges or restrictions must be the result of their not being willing to work at resolving their problem. Lifting of restrictions or returning privileges should be tied to their having committed to a specific plan to resolve their problem. Trying to control children by rewarding or punishing them not only doesn't teach responsible thinking, but, more importantly, it doesn't teach them how to creatively work at resolving their problems.

The Difficult Art of
Teaching Responsible Thinking

Although most of this has been already said in the body of this book, some things are worth repeating. The most important point to remember when dealing with children is that they are, like all of us, living control systems. They have their own wants and goals, they have their own uniquely created ways of perceiving the world, they make their own choices in trying to change their perceptions to the way they want things to be, and they have their own specific priorities.

Thus, dealing with children demands respect for their worlds, and, more importantly, understanding how best to help them work through the various difficulties and problems they have. Since all of their problems are internal and can only be understood by those having the problems, the way to help them deal with their conflicts is by asking them questions, not by telling them what you think.

The questioning process forces the parent or teacher to stay in the child's world. In Perceptual Control Theory terms, you're dealing with the children as individually and internally driven control systems, which is what they are. By asking the right questions, you're teaching children to deal with themselves in such a way as to satisfy their own internal goals. And you're teaching them to do this in the most effective way possible: to deal with the key elements of responsibility, namely, what they want, which is their goal; what the standards or rules are, which are what they base their choices on; what their specific choices and actions have been; and the consequences that flow from their decisions.

Ultimately, you get to the most crucial area, the responsibility questions: first, you ask them to compare (again, using Perceptual Contol Theory concepts) what they want to what they are doing, or what they're doing compared to what the rules or standards are, or what they're doing compared to other things they want; second, once they've accepted responsibility for their thinking in that area, you find out if they are willing to set a goal to work at resolving their problem — in Perceptual Contol Theory terms, you gauge the strength of the internal signal representing what they want relative to other wants. Once strongly committed to resolving their problems, children are ready to learn how to work out a plan to satisfy what they want with measurable goals and charts, as I discussed earlier.

As you can see, the Teacher-Parent Program is tied to a solid theoretical base, Perceptual Control Theory. It provides uniformity of standards in both home and school, and a way for parents and teachers to work cooperatively toward the goal of creating children who can think responsibly, which is the first necessary step toward acting responsibly. The following worksheet forms are used when teaching the parenting program. Many participants have used these forms, and some have suggested changes which have made the process easier and more efficient.

As I mentioned earlier, Form One can be used by parents with their children, and by couples who want to strengthen their relationships through the use of my quality time ideas. Form Two can be used by anyone who wants to make an effective plan or wants to teach another how to make a plan.

I use Form Three (page 193) when training participants to use the counseling techniques. I have them form into groups of three and take turns doing role-plays. One of them plays a child who either has been acting out in the playground, cafeteria, or classroom, or has been sent to a counselor or teacher with one of the many presenting problems of children who need counseling or who must be dealt with concerning a discipline problem. The second person plays the counselor, administrator, parent, or teacher. The person playing the monitor fills out the form, making sure that the person playing the counselor, parent, or teacher and who is doing the role-playing follows specifically the various rules and stages outlined on the form. This assures that the counseling strategy is maintained during the practice sessions.

Form Four (pages 194 and 195) was originally designed by Monte Silk, middle school principal at Sweetwater School District #2 in Green River, Wyoming. Monte took my ideas from several forms and combined them into a form which can be used by either a student, a teacher, or a parent. Together, we worked at revising this form during a week's workshop at the school; thus, we had constant feedback from the participants all week. A few weeks later, some suggestions were added during my workshops at the Shiawassee Regional School District near Durand, Michigan. On my second visit to the San Elizario School District, located a few miles east of El Paso, Texas, I discovered that Manuel Reyes, the assistant principal of the middle school, had devised his own version (Form Five, pages 196 and 197). I'm sure that by the time you look these forms over, other participants will have created their own forms or revised one of the forms I've mentioned.

Finally, a pocket-sized card is available which has my ideas on Love/Quality Time on one side and my ideas on Teaching Responsible Thinking on the other side. The latest revisions are shown on pages 59 and 149 of this book. This card can be obtained from Brandt Publishing.

PERFORMANCE PLAN FOR QUALITY TIME - FORM ONE
by Ed Ford & Associates

minutes
70
60
50
40
30
20
10

date->

instructions - *first*, set goal for number of minutes per day
              and run dotted line from the number of minutes
              you choose horizontally across
              second, write in dates beginning with today's
              date
              third, begin using the chart today and scotch
              tape to the bathroom mirror

List activities and time spent doing them each day

date   activity & time spent   date   activity & time spent

_____ _____   _____ _____

_____ _____   _____ _____

_____ _____   _____ _____

_____ _____   _____ _____

_____ _____   _____ _____

_____ _____   _____ _____

_____ _____   _____ _____

Teacher-Parent Program Copyright c 1992 Ed Ford & Assocs.

PERFORMANCE PLAN FOR IMPROVEMENT - FORM TWO
by Ed Ford & Associates

PERFORMANCE PLAN BY _____ Date _____

AN AREA OF NEEDED IMPROVEMENT: Explain what you are presently
doing and what you want to be doing in the future.

_____

_____

_____

_____

Measurable goal or standard: (must tie in to chart below)

_____

_____

Specific Action Plan: Detail what you are going to do to
achieve your goal (time, place, days, with whom, how long,
how many). Plan must contain specifics for measuring
progress over time.

_____

_____

_____

_____

_____

Measurable Goal Chart

Each person's initial _____Date _____

Next Meeting - Date _____ Time _____ Place _____

Teacher-Parent Program Copyright c 1992 Ed Ford & Assocs.

MONITOR RECORDING SHEET - FORM THREE
by Ed Ford & Associates

INSTRUCTIONS: When the counselor speaks, place a checkmark (✓) in the box that best describes the statement. Please note the special instructions when comparisons and commitments are asked.

		COUNSELOR	FIRST ROLE PLAY	SECOND ROLE PLAY
		asks - what are you doing		
		rules & standards		
	1. GATHER INFORMATION	choices & consequences		
		what do you want now		
		other information		
RESPONSIBILITY STAGES	2. COMPARE	*asks* client to compare actions with wants or rules	*write down comparison* _____ _____ _____ _____	*write down comparison* _____ _____ _____ _____
	3. COMMIT	*asks for* commitment	*write down commitment* _____ _____ _____ _____	*write down commitment* _____ _____ _____ _____
	4. PLAN	*teaches* client how to make a plan		
		ask them to compare plan to want and to commit to plan		

Teacher-Parent Program Copyright c 1992 Ed Ford & Assocs.

TEACHING RESPONSIBLE THINKING PLAN - FORM FOUR (PAGE 1)

Student Name _____ Date _____

I. ASK THE STUDENT....

GATHER INFORMATION
What would the teacher/parent say you were doing that placed you in the conference/time-out?

_____

What is it that you
wanted when you did this? _____
What were you doing
to get what you wanted? _____
What are the
rules and standards? _____
What are the various
choices you have now? _____

Explain the consequences that
result from making each choice? _____

What is it that
you want now? _____

II. TEACH RESPONSIBILITY

COMPARE   *circle your choice*
Is what you were doing against the rules or standards?   Yes or No
Is what you were doing getting you what you want?   Yes or No
Is what you were doing getting you all the things you want? Yes or No
COMMIT
Are you willing to work at resolving (fixing) your problem? Write your commitment

_____

III. HELP THE CLIENT MAKE A RESPONSIBLE PLAN

A. Establish measurable goal or standard. (Must tie to chart on page 2)

_____

B. Set specific action plan: Detail what you are going to do to achieve your goal (time, place, days, with whom, how long, how many). Plan must contain specifics for measuring progress over time.

_____

_____

_____

_____

_____

_____

TEACHING RESPONSIBLE THINKING - FORM FOUR (PAGE 2)

C. Compare and commit to plan.

Will this plan get what you want?   Circle Yes or No

Are you willing to commit to this plan? _____

IV. MEASURABLE GOAL CHART

To whom will you report
the progress of your plan? _____

How often? _____ When? _____ Where? _____

Student Signature _____

Counselor _____

Next meeting: Date _____ Time _____ Place _____

With whom? _____

Parent/Guardian Signature, if necessary _____

Please note: This sheet is a guideline for learning the process for
teaching responsible thinking. It does not include all questions,
techniques, or strategies used in working with clients.

CONTROL THEORY WORKSHEET - FORM FIVE (PAGE 1)   Name _____

Note: This form was created by Manuel Reyes, Assistant Principal, San
Elizario Middle School, San Elizario, Texas. It is another example of
the creative attempts by teachers and administrators to help both
parents and children in their schools.

I. GATHERING INFORMATION - In this stage, the counselor, whether it be
the student's principal, teacher, counselor, or parent, attempts to
establish what the student is presently doing, what rules were
violated, what the consequences are, what the student wants, and the
choices available to the student. Question to ask:

1. What is it that brought you here today? _____
*If student refuses to cooperate or gives you excuses, you repeat the
question until the student gives you a straight answer.
*If student persists in total innocence, ask student, *What would your
teacher say if he/she were here to explain the problem?*

2. Is there a rule for that particular behavior? _____
*If the student says, *NO, there is no rule for that,* then you can ask:
Is there an unwritten rule? If the student says: *I don't know what
you mean,* then ask: *Do other kids do the same thing you did, or do
they act differently?* If he or she responds *Yes,* then ask:

3. What is the rule? _____

4. What happens when you BREAK the rule? _____

5. Is that what you want? (refers to the consequences of breaking the

rule) _____

6. If breaking this rule is NOT getting you what you want, then what is
it you really WANT? (If student does not know, then you can provide
student with choices, e.g., to pass the class, to graduate, to stay out

of trouble.) _____

II. RESPONSIBILITY STAGES

A. COMPARE - Counselor attempts to compare what student is currently
doing to the rules or what he/she wants.

7. Is what you're doing NOW getting you what you want? _____

8. Is what you're doing against the rules? _____

B. COMMIT - Counselor attempts to get student to commit himself/herself
to resolving the problem.

9. Do you think you want to work at this? _____
*If student says YES, but attempts to attach conditions to it (*Yes, but
what are you going to do about the other students who are also doing the
same thing?*), you ask again. This time, however, you say: *Right now I
am only talking to YOU. Are you willing to work on this?*

10. Are you sure about this? You're sure? You're not just saying this

to get out of here -- are you? _____

C. INSTRUCTION - At this point, the counselor explains how a plan is
made AND what it will mean (you can refer to the outline of the plan).

CONTROL THEORY WORKSHEET - FORM FIVE (PAGE 2)

D. ACTION PLAN - What this amounts to is a written (or oral) plan to help student improve his/her behavior.

11. Area of Needed Improvement: Explain what you are currently doing and what you want to be doing in the future. _____

_____

12. What are you going to do about it? _____

_____

13. Measurable Goal or Standard: _____

_____

14. STUDENT RESPONSIBILITY PLAN: You must detail exactly what student will do to achieve the goal (timelines, place, days, with whom, how long, and how many).

A. What is the area of needed improvement? Explain what you are

presently doing and what you want to be doing in the future. _____

_____

_____

B. What measurable goal or standard do you hope to accomplish? _____

_____

C. SPECIFIC ACTION PLAN: Tell what you are going to do to achieve your goal (time, place, days, how long, how many). Plan must contain

specifics for measuring progress over time. _____

_____

_____

_____

D. MONITORING PROGRESS: How will the teacher/counselor/principal monitor student progress?

To whom will you report your progress with the plan? _____

How often? _____ When? _____ Where? _____

STUDENT SIGNATURE _____

TEACHER/COUNSELOR/PRINCIPAL SIGNATURE _____

Next Meeting: Date _____ Time _____ Place _____

With whom? _____

PARENT/GUARDIAN SIGNATURE, IF NECESSARY _____

MEASURABLE GOAL CHART

Appendix 3

PERCEPTUAL CONTROL THEORY RESOURCES

Greg Williams
CSG Archivist

The Control Systems Group

The CSG is a membership organization which supports the understanding of perceptual control systems. Academicians, clinicians, and other professionals in several disciplines, including biology, psychology, social work, economics, education, engineering, and sociology, are members of the Group. Annual meetings have been held since 1985. CSG publications include a series of books and the quarterly journal *Closed Loop* (see below).

For information on how to join, contact CSG, 73 Ridge Place, CR 510, Durango, CO 81301; phone (303)247-7986.

CSGnet

CSGnet is an electronic mail network for individuals interested in perceptual control theory. It is a lively forum for sharing ideas, asking questions, and learning more about the theory, its implications, and its problems.

There are no sign-up or connect-time charges for participation on CSGnet. The Internet address is CSG-L@VMD.CSO.UIUC.EDU and CSG-L@UIUCVMD is the Bitnet address. Messages sent to CSGnet via these addresses are automatically forwarded to more than 120 participants on five continents, as well as to hundreds of Net-News (Usenet) sites (newsgroup bit.listserv.csg-l). CSGnet also can be accessed via CompuServe, AT&T Mail, MCI Mail, or any other computer communication service with a gateway to Internet or Bitnet. For more information about subscribing to CSGnet, contact Gary Cziko, the network manager, at G-CZIKO@UIUC.EDU, phone him at (217)333-8527, or send a FAX to (217)244-7620.

"Threads" taken from some of the net's many conversations are printed in *Closed Loop*, sent to all CSG members. Some issues of *Closed Loop* also feature PCT research reports. Several back issues are available from CSG.

Videotapes

The 1993 CSG meeting was videotaped by Dag Forssell (23903 Via Flamenco, Valencia, CA 91355; phone (805)254-1195). He is selling a set of three tapes which shows most of the meeting.

"Love Guaranteed with Ed Ford," a 46-minute tape produced by PBS station KAET in Phoenix, is available for $21.95 postpaid from Brandt Publishing, 10209 N. 56th St., Scottsdale, AZ 85253.

Books Published by the CSG

All of the following are available from CSG Book Publishing, 460 Black Lick Rd., Gravel Switch, KY 40328; phone (606)332-7606.

Powers, William T. (1989). *Living control systems: Selected papers*.

Robertson, Richard J., and Powers, William T. (Eds.) (1990). *Introduction to modern psychology: The control-theory view*.

Marken, Richard S. (1992). *Mind readings: Experimental studies of purpose*.

Powers, William T. (1992). *Living control systems II: Selected papers*.

Other Books

Powers, William T. (1973). *Behavior: The control of perception*. Chicago: Aldine.

Gibbons, Hugh. (1977). *A theory of democracy*. Concord, New Hampshire, Franklin Pierce Law Center.

Petrie, Hugh G. (1981). *The dilemma of enquiry and learning.* Chicago and London: University of Chicago Press.

Plooij, Frans X. (1982). *The behavioral development of free-living chimpanzee babies and infants.* Norwood, New Jersey: Ablex.

Soldani, James C., and Ford, Edward E. (1984). *Money isn't enough: Managing people effectively using control system theory.* Revised edition. Scottsdale, Arizona: Ford-Soldani.

Robertson, Richard J. (1986). *Setting your own ego-stat: How to control your life instead of yourself.* Chicago: Robertson.

Ford, Edward E. (1987). *Love guaranteed: A better marriage in eight weeks.* San Francisco: Harper & Row.

Hershberger, Wayne A. (Ed.) (1989). *Volitional action: Conation and control.* Amsterdam: Elsevier Science (North-Holland).

Gibbons, Hugh. (1990). *The death of Jeffrey Stapleton: Exploring the way lawyers think.* Concord, New Hampshire: Franklin Pierce Law Center.

Runkel, Philip J. (1990). *Casting nets and testing specimens: Two grand methods of psychology.* New York, Westport, Connecticut, and London: Praeger.

McPhail, Clark. (1991). *The myth of the madding crowd.* Hawthorne, New York: Aldine de Gruyter.

Richardson, George P. (1991). *Feedback thought in social science and systems theory.* Philadephia: University of Pennsylvania Press.

Selected Papers

A comprehensive checklist of materials related to PCT, updated annually, is available for $5.00 postpaid from Greg Williams, 460 Black Lick Rd., Gravel Switch, KY 40328.

Powers, W. T., Clark, R. K., and McFarland, R. L. (1960). A general feedback theory of human behavior: Part I. *Perceptual and Motor Skills, 11*, 71-88.

Powers, W. T., Clark, R. K., and McFarland, R. L. (1960). A general feedback theory of human behavior: Part II. *Perceptual and Motor Skills, 11*, 309-323.

Powers, William T. (1973). Feedback: Beyond behaviorism. *Science, 179*, 351-356.

Powers, William T. (1976). Control-system theory and performance objectives. *Journal of Psycholinguistic Research, 5*, 285-297.

Powers, William T. (1978). Quantitative analysis of purposive systems: Some spadework at the foundations of scientific psychology. *Psychology Review, 85*, 417-435.

Powers, William T. (1978). A cybernetic model for research in human development. In M. N. Ozer (Ed.), *A cybernetic approach to the assessment of children: Toward a more humane use of human beings*, Boulder: Westview Press, 11-66.

Powers, William T. (1979). Degrees of freedom in social interactions. In Klaus Krippendorff (Ed.), *Communication and control in society*, New York, London, and Paris: Gordon and Breach, 267-278.

Powers, William T. (1979). The nature of robots: Part 1: Defining behavior. *BYTE, 4*(6), June, 132, 134, 136, 138, 140-141, 144.

Powers, William T. (1979). The nature of robots: Part 2: Simulated control system. *BYTE, 4*(7), July, 134-136, 138, 140, 142, 144, 146, 148-150.

Powers, William T. (1979). The nature of robots: Part 3: A closer look at human behavior. *BYTE, 4*(8), August, 94-96, 98, 100, 102-104, 106-108, 110-112, 114, 116.

Powers, William T. (1979). The nature of robots: Part 4: Looking for controlled variables. *BYTE*, *4*(9), September, 96, 98-102, 104, 106-110, 112.

Marken, Richard. (1980). The cause of control movements in a tracking task. *Perceptual and Motor Skills*, *51*, 755-758.

Powers, William T. (1980). A systems approach to consciousness. In Julian M. Davidson and Richard J. Davidson (Eds.), *The psychology of consciousness*, New York and London: Plenum Press, 217-242.

Marken, Richard. (1982). Intentional and accidental behavior: A control theory analysis. *Psychological Reports*, *50*, 647-650.

McCord, David M. (1982). Control theory: Overview and empirical demonstration. *Alabama Studies in Psychology*, *1*(1), Fall, 7-16.

Marken, Richard. (1983). "Mind reading": A look at changing intentions. *Psychological Reports*, *53*, 267-270.

Powers, William T. (1984). Interactionism and control theory. In Joseph R. Royce and Leendert P. Mos (Eds.), *Annals of Theoretical Psychology*, Volume 2, New York and London: Plenum Press, 355-358.

Marken, Richard S. (1985). Selection of consequences: Adaptive behavior from random reinforcement. *Psychological Reports*, *56*, 379-383.

Marken, Richard S. (1986). Perceptual organization of behavior: A hierarchical control model of coordinated action. *Journal of Experimental Psychology: Human Perception and Performance*, *12*, 267-276.

McPhail, Clark, and Wohlstein, Ronald T. (1986). Collective locomotion as collective behavior. *American Sociological Review*, *51*, 447-463.

Marken, Richard S. (1988). The nature of behavior: Control as fact and theory. *Behavioral Science, 33,* 196-206.

Marken, Richard S., and Powers, William T. (1989). Random-walk chemotaxis: Trial-and-error as a control process. *Behavioral Neuroscience, 103,* 1348-1355.

Bourbon, W. Thomas. (1990). Invitation to the dance: Explaining the variance when control systems interact. *American Behavioral Scientist, 34*(1), September/October, 95-105.

Bourbon, W. Thomas, Copeland, Kimberly E., Dyer, Vick R., Harman, Wade K., and Mosley, Barbara L. (1990). On the accuracy and reliability of predictions by control-system theory. *Perceptual and Motor Skills, 71,* 1331-1338.

Ford, Edward E. (1990). On understanding control theory: Learning some difficult concepts. *American Behavioral Scientist, 34*(1), September/October, 117-118.

Goldstein, David M. (1990). Clinical applications of control theory. *American Behavioral Scientist, 34*(1), September/October, 110-116.

Marken, Richard S. (1990). A science of purpose. *American Behavioral Scientist, 34*(1), September/October, 1-94.

McPhail, Clark, and Tucker, Charles W. (1990). Purposive collective action. *American Behavioral Scientist, 34*(1), September/October, 81-94.

Pavloski, Raymond P., Barron, Gerard T., and Hogue, Mark A. (1990). Reorganization: Learning and attention in a hierarchy of control systems. *American Behavioral Scientist, 34*(1), September/October, 32-54.

Plooij, Frans X., and van de Rijt-Plooij, H. C. (1990). Developmental transitions as successive reorganizations of a control hierarchy. *American Behavioral Scientist, 34*(1), September/October, 67-80.

Powers, William T. (1990). Control theory: A model of organisms. *System Dynamics Review*, *6*(1), Winter, 1-20.

Powers, William T. (1990). Control theory and statistical generalizations. *American Behavioral Scientist*, *34*(1), September/October, 24-31.

Runkel, Philip J. (1990). Research method for control theory. *American Behavioral Scientist*, *34*(1), September/October, 14-23.

Williams, William D. (1990). The Giffen effect: A note on economic purposes. *American Behavioral Scientist*, *34*(1), September/October, 106-109.

Marken, Richard S. (1991). Degrees of freedom in behavior. *Psychological Science*, *2*, 92-100.

Powers, William T. (1991). Commentary on Bandura's "human agency." *American Psychologist*, *46*, 151-153.

Cziko, Gary A. (1992). Purposeful behavior as the control of perception: Implications for educational research. *Educational Researcher*, *21*(9), December, 10-18, 27.

McPhail, Clark, Powers, William T., and Tucker, Charles W. (1992). Simulating individual and collective action in temporary gatherings. *Social Science Computer Review*, *10*, 1-28.